MIGHTY MISSISSIPPI

MIGHTY MISSISSIPPI

BIOGRAPHY OF A RIVER

MARQUIS W. CHILDS

Foreword by Geoffrey C. Ward

TICKNOR & FIELDS

New Haven and New York

1982

Library of Congress Cataloging in Publication Data

Childs, Marquis William, 1903–
  Mighty Mississippi.

  1. Mississippi River — History. 2. Mississippi River — Description and travel. 3. Mississippi River Valley — History. 4. Mississippi River Valley — Description and travel. 5. Childs, Marquis William, 1903–   . I. Title.
F351.C47   977   82-3299
ISBN 0-89919-088-X   AACR2

Designed by John O. C. McCrillis
Map by John O. C. McCrillis

Printed in the United States of America

S 10 9 8 7 6 5 4 3 2

In memory of my daughter Malissa Childs Elliott
and my brother Henry Richard Childs

Contents

Foreword

Eighty years ago, in the soft Missouri spring of 1902, Mark
Twain came home to Hannibal for the last time. He stayed five
days, greeting childhood friends now bent with age, and visiting
his old house. "It all seems so small to me," he said. "I suppose if
I should come back here ten years from now it would be the size
of a birdhouse." He spoke to Sunday-school classes, dined with a
childhood sweetheart, stout and fitted with false teeth, and
handed out diplomas at high-school commencement: "Take one.
Pick out a good one. Don't take two, but be sure you get a good
one." And he walked with an old friend up Holliday's Hill—
Cardiff Hill in *Tom Sawyer*. "That is one of the loveliest sights I
ever saw," he said, gazing across the broad river toward the Illinois shore. "Down there by the island is the place we used to
swim, and yonder is where a man was drowned, and there's
where the steamboat sank. Down there . . . is where the Millerites
put on their robes one night to go to heaven. None of them went
that night, but I suppose most of them have gone by now."
Crowds followed him everywhere, and gathered on the depot
platform to say a noisy good-bye. Then, above the cheering and
the chuffing of the train, he heard the unmistakable voice of his
old schoolmate Tom Nash, bellowing in a deaf man's oblivious
whisper, "Same damned fools, Sam. Same damned fools."

The next year, another son of the Mississippi was born, in the
river town of Clinton, Iowa. Like Mark Twain, Marquis Childs
became a newspaperman. As correspondent and columnist he
covered Washington for five decades, winning the very first Pu-
litzer Prize for commentary in 1969, and somehow finding the
time to write or edit sixteen books along the way.

But like Twain, too, he never managed to wash the memory of life along the great river from his mind. This book is the happy result. Begun at the dawn of Franklin Roosevelt's New Deal, then put away for half a century, it is too modestly subtitled. It is far more than a "biography" of a river. Mr. Childs tells this extraordinary, sweeping story of American exploration and settlement and enterprise beautifully, crowded as it is with deft sketches of such diverse characters as La Salle and Jay Gould, Abraham Lincoln and Russell Long.

But he also offers a vividly evocative look at one river town, Winslow, Iowa, as it was in the 1930s, when the Mississippi's glory days were already a dimming memory. In its poignant, very different way, this portrait of a dreaming, dying town can stand comparison with Twain's Hannibal.

And running underneath all of the book, history and reporting alike, there is a steady undercurrent of struggle between the mighty river and generation after generation of men who have tried to tame it in the interests of commerce or safety, transport or sheer stubborn pride. Mr. Childs observes the ebb and flow of this endless war with an ironist's eye: his money is clearly on the river, and I suspect he believes Mark Twain's old friend Tom Nash had it about right.

GEOFFREY C. WARD
Editor, *American Heritage*

Introduction

I began to write this book in 1932, when I was twenty-nine years old. Growing up on the banks of the great river I had explored the history of its turbulent life and had seen at first hand its slow decline. In the river as I had known it there was both promise and threat — floods reaching the level of the streets, storms sweeping the valley with cannonading of thunder and lightning, and the promise of the passionate advocates of a river commerce reborn by way of the federal treasury.

The river was almost empty. Except for a rare excursion steamer or a federal boat tending the channel, it was a silent expanse of water, a mile or so from shore to shore. There were those who believed that one day trade and traffic would be restored and the river would teem with life again. The apostle of this faith in our town was a doughty, gnarled fellow named Halleck Seaman who, if you gave him the time, would talk endlessly about the great river, its glorious past and its certain renaissance. Only a few years earlier the surge of the rafting boom had lighted up every town on the upper Mississippi.

Although I did not entirely subscribe to the doctrine of Halleck Seaman, I was tempted, if only by the legendary past. This was colored by a feeling of "ours and theirs." The river was ours, the railroads were theirs, the property of distant possessors who we could not know or restrain.

The lore of the Mississippi, the feel of it, was in my bones. Going up and down the river to New Orleans, I was pleased to think that the city held something of the past I was exploring. I spent many hours in the historical museum and library in the Cabildo. It was presided over by Miss Beauregard, daughter of the Confederate general, who was unfailingly kind and helpful, and rich in her own background of the city's past, which she shared with an upstart northerner. With a friend I went by canoe from Saint Paul to my home town of Lyons, which was later absorbed into Clinton, Iowa. We slept on sandbars as empty of life as the river itself. The archives of the Mississippi Historical Society in Saint Louis stored the records of a hundred years. And now and then I came upon an old-timer with a vivid memory of past glory.

But the federal government, through Franklin Roosevelt's Public Works Administration, stepped in to try to master the Mississippi at a huge cost not alone in money but in the disruption of the whole course of nature throughout the valley. I put the manuscript aside and turned to journalism in the Washington bureau of the *St. Louis Post-Dispatch*.

Now it is time to complete the story, including the last round of the conflict between the railroads and the river — a conflict that developed a new ferocity in 1980. Finishing my account after so long an interval, I like to think it reflects the vigor, the passion, the love of life, of that mighty stream.

MIGHTY MISSISSIPPI

1

Wilderness

Although their ideas of distance were European, the men of the sixteenth and seventeenth centuries had nevertheless some appreciation of the fabulous extent of the American wilderness. It grew through the two centuries of exploration with a quality fantastic, almost dreamlike, as one prince after another heard the distressing news from the Americas of disaster, catastrophe, and defeat. They persisted as long as they could in the belief that this land was only a minor obstruction on the trade route to China, sending one unhappy expedition after another to find a passage through this narrow strip of land. At last they accepted, with a faint, perplexed irritation, the fact that America was an all but empty continent of limitless extent.

The Spaniards, more than all other peoples, were disillusioned in North America. They came from the golden adventure of Mexico and Peru, swollen with riches and arrogance. It was only gold that they wanted, and with the extraordinary oneness of view of which the Spanish are capable, they blundered through the wilderness in search of it — first Narváez, and then Coronado and de Soto.

For all their fearful suffering, one cannot help but be a little amused at the spectacle they made. They were like angry children in a rage at the sun or the moon, these gentlemen adventurers stumbling through swamp and forest with their futile armies burdened with worse than futile armor. They were beset by fever, hunger, and the constant hostility of the Indians, whom they slaughtered and enslaved with casual cruelty. Every plague of the wilderness, great and small, fell upon them: clouds of midges; showers of arrows; violent storms; dysentery, and death, prolonged and painful.

The river to de Soto was accidental, irrelevant, a perilous crossing to be got over — that and no more. He came upon it one day in the early spring of 1541, at the end of a seven-day march from the camp in northern Mississippi where the party had spent an irksome and dreary winter. The Gentleman of Elvas relates that this river, which they called Rio Grande, was "half a league over, so that a man could not be distinguished from one side to the other; it was very deep and very rapid, and being always full of trees and timber that was carried down by the force of the stream, the water was thick and very muddy." Having crossed the great river, they floundered northward through the muddy bottomlands. Later, a rare friendship developed between the Spaniards and the savages, and de Soto bought two wives, sisters of the chief, for a shirt.

Aimlessly the explorers went on through the forest and over the barren prairie and the difficult upland, first north and then south, making camp in the valley of the Washita, perhaps two hundred miles west of the Mississippi. The winter that followed was a miserable one — terribly cold and damp and marked by a gnawing sense of despair by these children lost in the vast dark continent of America. Two hundred and fifty men had died, and one hundred and fifty horses, since they had left their ships. How many days' march away the sea was no one knew any longer. They were becoming, as de Soto's iron will yielded before the fever that ravaged his body, a mob in flight. At the Mississippi again, de Soto sent a party of men to seek a way of escape along the bank of the river. They returned at the end of eight days to report that travel was all but impossible because of the bayous, marshes, and dense forest. Unable to face the defeat of his high hopes, de Soto died of the fever that had wracked him so long.

The 21 of May departed out of this life, the valorous, virtuous, and valient Captaine, Don Fernando de Soto, Gou-

vernour of Cuba, and Adelantado of Florida; whom fortune advanced as it useth to doe others, that he might have the higher fall. He departed in such a place, and at such a time, as in his sicknesse he had but little comfort: and the danger wherein all his people were of perishing in that Countrie, which appeared before their eyes was cause sufficient, why every one of them had need of comfort, and why they did not visit nor accompanie him as they ought to have done.

So Richard Hakluyt translated the *Relation of the Gentleman of Elvas.* Two months later the gaunt, half-naked remnant of de Soto's army reached Tampico and, falling upon the familiar earth of this Spanish town, "remained untiring in giving thanks to God."

For a century the wilderness was quiet, peopled only by the Indians, who disturbed it as little as the bears and the bobcats. In Europe there was still no conception of its scope. Cartographers scratched a vague river that led into a vaguer sea upon their maps. The dream of a western empire recurred to trouble councils of state. But the defeat of the Spaniards had been so crushing that few explorers cared to venture beyond the coast.

From the first, the French showed themselves more suited to life in the wilds. They brought from the maritime provinces a seafaring skill and endurance combined with a peasant patience and perseverance. Samuel de Champlain went about establishing his colony on the rock of Quebec with care and a considerable understanding of the needs of this new country. The Jesuits followed him, and their way was illumined by the intense fervor of their mission.

Although they had not ventured to penetrate its mysteries, the men of western Europe had never ceased to be stirred by the idea of the New World, its great river, the sea that should lead to China, the persistent cities of gold. Poets and schoolboys and soldiers and old men were moved to wonder by this idea. Now the accounts that the Jesuits sent back quickened imagination anew. The theme of the river occurred over and over, the mysterious river that was itself as broad as a sea, the great river that

must empty into the South Sea. Marc Lescarbot wrote a sonnet
to Champlain:

> *Car d'un fleuve infine tu cherches l'origine,*
> *Afin qu'à l'avenir y faisant ton séjour*
> *Tu nous fasses par là parvenir à la Chine.*

It was a stubborn illusion, the "infinite river" that bore down
toward the Indies. Seeking this western passage to the sea of
China, Champlain in 1634 sent adventurer Jean Nicolet on a
voyage of exploration, guided by seven Indians, up the Ottawa
River and through the Lakes to Green Bay in Lake Michigan. It
was the farthest point west that any white man had reached in
the north. Nicolet had the foresight to take with him a Chinese
gown of damask "all strewn with flowers and birds of many
colors" so that, according to Francis Parkman's interpretation,
he should not appear too eccentric in his dress among the Chinese.

This he put on to delight the Winnebagos who gathered in
large numbers on the shore of the bay. When he fired his gun for
them, they fell down in awe before the god who carried thunder
in his hands. At the terrific sound the women and children fled
into the woods, as generation after generation were to do for at
least two centuries. Ascending the Fox River, which empties into
Green Bay, Nicolet came to the country of the Algonquin Ma-
scotins, a people whose speech he readily understood. Off to the
south, they told him, was "a great water." From the Fox there
was a three-day portage to another river, which was tributary to
the "great water." But Nicolet turned back. It is assumed he was
satisfied to have been so close to the Sea of China and decided
that in gaining this knowledge he had fulfilled his mission, for
the Indians spoke of it as a sea, and he needed no more than that
to stir all the images of the coveted trade route to the countries of
myrrh and spice and precious jewels. Returning through the
Lakes, he reached the Ottawa River in time to join a trading
party traveling to Quebec. He had been gone just a year.

Priest and trader were penetrating ever deeper into the wilds.
The one sought to save the savage's soul and the other to buy the

savage's beaver skins, yet they somehow complemented each other. Unfortunately, the harvest of souls remained all but negligible, while the beaver trade flourished and returned to French merchants enough revenue to stir a practical interest in what Louis XIV called "that patch of snow." In their approach to the wilderness and the Indians, the French were above all things practical. They did not assume the role of conquistadores demanding cities of gold of a primitive people. They accepted the Indian for what he was, adopting his ways of travel, discovering his cunning in the forest, respecting his fortitude and strange, dour sagacity. Priests, voyageurs, *coureurs des bois* made their way along the Indian paths, down the lakes, up the rivers, and the wilderness closed in behind them, leaving little trace of their stealthy passage.

Even the fascination of the "great water" could not lure them beyond the bounds of what was discreet and cautious. Like Jean Nicolet, they turned back, prudent and dutiful. Here a rumor and there a report from out of the forest fed the imagination. The *Jesuit Relation* of 1654 speaks of the sea separating America from China as being only nine days distant from Green Bay, a narrow sea and easy of passage. Chouart Groseilliers and Pierre Radisson, two traders who spent the winter of 1658 to 1659 on the southern shores of Lake Superior, brought from the Sioux Indians word of a river of fabulous extent. It was Father Allouez, founder of the mission of Pointe du Saint Esprit in 1665, who first sent out the name "Missipi."

Knowledge became more nearly exact. Father Allouez went farther than Nicolet. With Father Dablon he ascended the Fox and portaged to the head of the Wisconsin. But although he knew, as Nicolet had not known, that the Wisconsin led into the great river, he, too, turned back, recording in his journal that it was only a six-day journey from the point he had reached to the "Messisipi." And now the *Jesuit Relation* for 1669 to 1670 set it down that the "Messisipi" was more than a league wide, that it flowed from north to south, that the Indians had never traveled to its mouth, that it was still doubtful whether it emptied into the Gulf of Florida or the Gulf of California.

This was very close. Three years later Father Marquette, who
had replaced Father Allouez at Pointe du Saint Esprit, set out
with a trader named Louis Joliet from Mackinaw on a voyage of
exploration. Under the direction of Louis XIV and his forceful
minister, Colbert, the government of New France had been
changed. For the first time since Champlain there was a real interest in discovery. As Nicolet had done, the party of Marquette
and Joliet went up the Fox River. Following the course of Father
Allouez and Father Dablon, they portaged to the Wisconsin.
Passing down the Wisconsin, they reached the Mississippi on
June 17, 1673.

They floated leisurely on the broad stream. At a village of the
Illinois Indians they were warned that the river below swarmed
with monsters, and Father Marquette seems to have been half
inclined to believe them, for he wrote: "We met from time to
time monstrous fish, which struck so violently against our canoes
that at first we took them to be large trees which threatened to
upset us. We saw also a hideous monster; his head was like that
of a tiger, his nose was sharp, and somewhat resembled a wildcat;
his beard was long, his ears stood upright, the color of his head
was gray, and his neck black. He looked upon us for some time,
but as we came near him our oars frightened him away."

After they had passed the mouth of the Arkansas River, they
came upon increasing evidence of the influence of the Spanish.
For the first time the two spheres of exploitation, north and
south, touched, at the remote periphery of each. The wilderness
would pass away, and swiftly. In one village the French found an
iron cooking pot; in another, a few words of Spanish, remembered magic; in still another, a store of gaudy trinkets of European origin adorning the chief. Fear of capture by the Spaniards,
dread of the long homeward journey, and the assurance of the
Indians that the mouth of the Mississippi was only ten days distant to the south caused them to turn back.

Full of all the marvels they had seen — the roaring, boiling
influx of the Missouri, the clear limpidity of the Ohio, the fearful
creatures painted on the bluff at Piasa, the mysterious mounds
that loomed above the bank — they faced northward, proud of

the success of their errand. And they may well have taken pride in their knowledge, for they would correct one of the most persistent geographical illusions. No map maker could henceforth place China beyond the line of the Great Lakes. Imagination could no longer twist the Mississippi into a westward direction and the Gulf of California. If it was more nearly thirty days to the mouth and the Gulf of Mexico from the point at which they had stopped, that was a minor error in the impressive report they made at Quebec.

It was important that the river was no longer a mirage, no longer the symbol of a vague and futile dream. It was seen to be one of the great rivers of the earth, with tributaries of seemingly incredible extent, draining a vast area of forest and prairie that abounded with all natural riches. Through the slow channels of European information these facts gradually penetrated. But it remained for still another adventurer to appreciate the significance of this highway at the heart of a continent.

Robert Cavelier de La Salle's attitude toward the New World was in almost every respect a modern one, far in advance of his time. He takes rank as one of the foremost figures in the discovery and settlement of America. It would seem that almost from the first he was free from the childlike outlook which held that the Americas were a brief, opulent prize to be seized for what they might momentarily yield to a depleted treasury. There is high tragedy in his long struggle, grim heartbreak in the misfortunes that constantly beset him. Through the endless conflict — with indifference, with shallow greed, with intriguing and jealous rivals — he never lost sight of his river and what it might mean to France. It became an obsession, almost a kind of madness. Or so they thought at Versailles, seeing this stern, hard-bitten man from out of the wilds.

His family were Rouen merchants, good, respectable people who had built up a comfortable fortune in the trade of wool. He studied to be a Jesuit, then changed his mind and left the order — a bad thing to do if one were to develop later ambitions for another kind of career, or so it was thought then, and so La Salle himself believed. Perhaps he caught his desire for exploration out of the *Jesuit Relation,* the yearbook that recited the latest adventures of the missionaries in the Americas. Or he may have gone to New France, when he had finally left the Jesuit order, in the despair of an all but penniless young outcast.

Once there, he was quick to acquire the skills of forest and stream, and when Joliet returned to Quebec with the stirring news of his explorations, La Salle seized upon the idea of the river. He returned to France by the next ship to get money for an expedition, for large boats to navigate the river, for the establishment of permanent trading posts. He bore a letter of commendation from the governor of New France, his steadfast friend Comte de Frontenac, to the powerful Jean Baptiste Colbert: "I can but recommend to you, Monseigneur, the Sieur de La Salle, on his way to France, a man of audacity and intelligence and the most capable I know of here for all the enterprises and discoveries which one might wish to confide to him, having a very perfect knowledge of the state of the country, as will be apparent to you if you will be good enough to give him a few minutes' audience."

By means of a bribe, La Salle gained access to the presence of Colbert and called upon that rich store of eloquence which, although ordinarily a reserved man, he could invariably summon in behalf of his schemes for the river. Colbert got for him from Louis two patents — one a grant to Forte Frontenac on the upper Saint Lawrence, the other conferring upon him the title of gentleman and the right to bear arms, designated as a black shield embossed with a running greyhound in silver and an eight-point star in gold. From his family and friends he got money for his project, in exchange for a promise of great profit from the fur trade at Fort Frontenac.

Back in Quebec, his brother, the Abbé Jean Cavelier, tried to dissuade him from the voyage of discovery. The practical business was Fort Frontenac. Under proper management that should yield twenty-five thousand *livres* a year. But no sum of money, nothing, could have deflected La Salle, who continued to make most careful plans for his expedition. Delegating his authority at Fort Frontenac, he sent out an advance party to begin building an outpost at Niagra. Fear of the Jesuits preyed upon his mind. He wrote back to France: "My enterprise disturbs the commerce of certain people who will scarcely tolerate it. They hoped to make of this region a new Paraguay and the way which I bar to them facilitated an advantageous correspondence with Mexico. This barrier will infallibly mortify them and you know how they are toward those who resist them."

In that first expedition one may see the pattern of painful adversity. La Salle may well have believed that his enemies directed the powers of air, earth, fire, and water. There is hardly space to recount his failures: the loss of the schooner *Griffin*, which he had launched with such hope on Lake Erie; the treachery, and worse, the stupidity, of his men; the interminable waiting in the squalid, lousy huts of the Illinois; the overturned canoes and the loss of supplies and irreplaceable tools; the annoying officiousness of Father Hennepin; the slow, tedious journeys alone through the wilderness in search of deserters and laggards; the infinite patience with which the Indians had to be met. As some compensation for these and many, many other trials, there was the rare, precious loyalty of one companion, Henry de Tonty, a friend who never lost faith. La Salle established Fort Crèvecoeur on the Illinois River, but at a fearful cost in money and time.

It was not until he had won out in a long struggle with his creditors at Quebec, who had all but ruined him in his absence, that he was able to equip another, more modest, expedition. In February he first came out onto his river. Broken ice floated thick over its surface, threatening the fragile canoes, but such a minor obstacle could scarcely hinder this man. He headed south with sure determination, at a swift, even pace. The air was kinder. There were flowers, red as fire, blooming in the trees — flowers that scented the air with heavy, strange perfume. A tribe of southern Indians, the Tensas, lived in houses made of clay; one of the chief's wives wore a necklace of pearls. On and on they passed by the endless canebrakes. The water tasted brackish. Then at last they came out upon the open sea.

On the 8th we reascended the river, a little above its confluence with the sea, to find a dry place beyond the reach of
inundations. The elevation of the North Pole was here about
27. Here we prepared a column and a cross, and to the said
column were affixed the arms of France, with this inscrip-
tion:

"LOUIS LE GRAND, ROI DE FRANCE ET DE NAVARRE,
RÈGNE; LE NEUVIÈME AVRIL, 1682."

The whole party, under arms, chanted the Te Deum, the
Exaudiat, the Domine salvum fac Regem; and then, after a
salute of fire arms and cries of *Vive le Roi,* the column was
erected by M. de la Salle, who, standing near it, said, with a
loud voice in French: "In the name of the most high,
mighty, invincible, and victorious Prince, Louis the Great,
by the Grace of God King of France and Navarre, Four-
teenth of that name, this ninth day of April, one thousand
six hundred and eighty-two, I, in virtue of the commission
of his Majesty which I hold in my hand, and which may be
seen by all to whom it may concern, have taken and do now
take, in the name of his Majesty and of his successors to the
crown, possession of this country of Louisiana, the seas,
harbors, ports, bays, adjacent straits; and all the nations,
people, provinces, cities, towns, villages, mines, minerals,
fisheries, streams, and rivers, comprised in the extent of the
said Louisiana, from the mouth of the great river. . . .

La Salle, and perhaps La Salle alone, knew the value of this
world he had taken for Louis. He understood that it was necessary to establish colonies in the south in order for the mother
country to benefit from the natural resources of the vast region
he had just passed through; he knew that the south would yield a
far richer harvest than the north, frozen and isolated for so many
months. The long way back — the Mississippi, the Illinois, the
Lakes, the Saint Lawrence, Quebec, the ocean voyage — and he
faced once more the gilded arrogance of Versailles. How little
must this kingdom have seemed to him; the tight little European

snuffbox, with the painted image of the grand monarch at the center. And how strangely must his eagerness have fallen upon their ears.

"We should obtain everything which has enriched New England and Virginia . . . timber of every kind, salted meat, tallow, corn, sugar, tobacco, honey, wax, resin, and other gums . . . immense pasturages . . . a prodigious number of buffaloes, stags, hinds, roes, bears, otters, lynxes . . . hides and furs . . . there are cotton, cochineal nuts, turnsoles . . . entire forests of mulberry trees . . . slate, coal, vines, apple-trees. . . ."

But this was so much breath wasted. The key to the French snuffbox, as La Salle soon discovered, lay in the passionate national jealousies — and in particular in Louis's jealousy of Spain — that kept the continent in almost constant war. This, adroitly used — in the argument that a colony planted on the shores of the Gulf of Mexico would serve as the first wedge to split Spain's empire in the Americas — unlocked the treasury. La Salle was to have ships, arms, supplies. Men and women in one desperate plight or another were pressed into the rolls of the new colony, or they were lured by the dream of fabulous wealth. The squadron sailed from La Rochelle in July of 1684.

La Salle's colony was a grim failure, beset by misfortune from its wretched beginnings to its miserable end. Treacherously deserted on a barren stretch of sand by the commander of the squadron, the colonists established Fort Saint Louis, in which they died of fever, sun stroke, starvation, and Indian forays. La Salle had lost his river.

Three times during the years 1685 to 1687 he struck out from the dwindling colony in search of the river, knowing that if he did not find it and get help from the French in Canada they all should die. On the last search he was a man lost to hope; his face was without expression, numbed as though with the frost of northern winters; his eyes were withdrawn and blank. He and his party wore sailcloth clothes; they had no shoes. Rivers swollen with the spring rise were crossed in improvised boats of skin. Quarreling broke out among the men, in which the leader took little part. Those who were most disaffected plotted to kill him.

As he walked down a trail to discover why the plotters had stayed behind, they shot him down and he died within an hour.

No Frenchman of La Salle's stature was ever again concerned with the colonization of America. After the custom of the time, the French deposited colonies along the Mississippi River. Pierre Lemoyne d' Iberville and Jean Baptiste le Moyne, sieur de Bienville, established New Orleans, which for many years was a weak and pewling sort of place forever in need of sustenance from the homeland. In the country of the Illinois the French from Canada met the French from the south and founded Kaskaskia, Fort Chartres, Cahokia, and, a little later, in 1735, Sainte Genevieve on the west bank of the river. These last were at least hardy and self-supporting. Very early in the history of the French settlements they sent down supplies to New Orleans: flour, bacon, pork, leather, lumber, wine, tallow, lead, hides and peltries in keelboats and bateaux.

The river was still to a large degree a lost river, a long, shining, empty expanse with, here and there, remote little collections of huts — they were hardly more than that. The French had a way of building that was called "cat and clay": they set up posts two feet apart, joined like a ladder, with a stake between, and then worked up moss and mud in rolls "as big as a man's leg and two feet long"; these they threw over the stakes and smoothed all down, making a solid wall. Years rolled by, like the indifferent river, with only a flood or a drought or an Indian powwow to mark the passing of time. The French on the Mississippi were not conquerors. They were petite bourgeoisie and peasant farmers who placated the Indians, mixed with them, and married them.

When France turned her treasury over to the Scotch financier John Law, and his Mississippi System, the settlements enjoyed a sudden growth. During this period vessels arrived frequently from France, bearing settlers and munitions. On August 24, 1720, "arrived on board the *St. Andre* 260 men. On the 3rd of September, the *Profond* with 240 men. On the 10th, the *Marin* with 186. On the 20th, on board the *Loire* 156. On the 14th December on board the *Elephant* 250. . . . About this time arrived many vessels from Africa with slaves, and from France with pas-

sengers." The boom brought eight hundred new settlers to Cahokia and Kaskaskia; stone mills and storehouses were built
there. But Law overissued his paper currency, and when the
Mississippi bubble burst he fled to Venice and the settlements
lapsed into their former quiescence.

It was an extremely simple, almost primitive life, with occasional rare amenities, a dance or a visit from the agent of the governor, to remind the settlers of what they had left. The dress of
these transplanted bourgeois was remarkably plain. The men
wore heavy cotton or gingham pants, without the support of sus-
penders but fastened by a belt and clasp around the waist; a blue
or colored shirt with no vest; a white mackinaw blanket with a
capuchin, and moccasins. The apparel of the women was sim-
plicity itself. Their dresses were of plain cotton or calico; man-
telets adorned their shoulders and breasts; their necks were covered with rich madras handkerchiefs, and their feet with
moccasins. The old of both sexes wore blue or madras handkerchiefs about their heads.

And yet profound changes were taking place. The wilderness
was being prepared for the transformation that was to come. The
fur traders, the voyageurs, the illegal *coureurs des bois* were going
everywhere, paddling up even the smallest streams, finding ways
through the densest forests. The dispute over the fur trade between the British on Hudson's Bay and the French on the Saint
Lawrence sent traders and voyageurs down into the upper Mississippi valley. Here and there a post was formed, such as Prairie
du Chien at the mouth of the Wisconsin, to become a settlement
by the slow accumulation of men who were too old or too weary
to follow the trade, women, and Indian stragglers. Julien Dubuque and others came to scratch for lead along the Fever River
and on the bluffs that towered above the Mississippi. Here they
were even more remote from France and the conventions of the
past than in the South. The following is from a history of the
early settlements:

In speaking of the early settlers, and their marriage connections, I should perhaps explain a little. In the absence of

religious instructions, and it becoming so common to see the Indians use so little ceremony about marriage, the idea of a verbal matrimonial contract became familiar to the early French settlers, and they generally believed that such a contract was valid without any other ceremony. . . . A woman of Prairie du Chien, respectable in her class, told me that she was attending a ball in the place, and that a trader, who resided on the Lower Mississippi, had his canoe loaded to leave as soon as the ball was over, proposed to marry her; and as he was a trader and ranked above her, she was pleased with the offer, and as his canoe was waiting, he would not delay for further ceremony. She stepped from the ball-room on board his canoe, and went with him down the Mississippi, and they lived together three or four years, and she had two children by him. She assured me that she then believed herself as much the wife of this man as if she had been married with all the ceremony of the most civilized communities, and was not convinced to the contrary, until he unfeelingly abandoned her and married another; and from her manner of relating it, I believed her sincere.

If the Indians thus had some influence on the whites, the latter revolutionized many phases of savage life. The Indians abandoned their century-old ways in an amazingly short time and became entirely dependent upon trade. French-made axes and knives of iron supplanted stone and copper implements; bows and arrows were abandoned for European firearms. The traders taught the Indians to make bullets from the lead of the Galena district. Blankets replaced hides, iron and copper kettles the old friable pottery. Porcelain beads took the place of wampum, laboriously fashioned from clam shells, as currency. The copper or stone amulet was discarded for bangles, bracelets, and nose rings from Paris. Imported paints adorned the naked Indians with patterns more exotic than primitive colors from the earth allowed. These changes took place within less than a decade after the arrival of the trader in the Indian community.

Today, with the world bound together in an inescapable intimacy, it is difficult to realize how little the events of what is by agreement called history touched the people of the river. News took as many years as it now takes seconds to reach these outposts. A ship would appear in New Orleans to spread some startling information through the town, word of what had happened two or three years before on the Atlantic seaboard. A canoe would be sighted on the river and the settlers would gather in the town square to hear a proclamation or a dispatch. The memory of this might endure for a few weeks or for a few months and then grow dim before the reality of crops and furs.

After 1763, when France lost the war with the British in America, many of the French moved to the west side of the Mississippi to escape English rule, and so Saint Louis was founded. Fort Chartres was abandoned. Kaskaskia dwindled. Word that France had ceded Louisiana to Spain caused a short-lived indignation. It was too far away to matter, and the common man, who peopled these parts, had never concerned himself over rule or authority so long as he was left unmolested in his work.

The War of the Revolution had some slight reverberation on the banks of the Mississippi. George Rogers Clark, with a band of followers recruited from Virginia and the neighborhood of Pittsburgh, took Kaskaskia and persuaded the French that their safety was with him. Assured by the village priest that Clark was their savior, they showed their joy by "addorning the streets with flowers and pavilians of different colors, compleating their happiness by singing, etc." Clark and his men took Vincennes, too, and defended Saint Louis from the attack of the British and Indians from Detroit. It was of great strategic importance that this part of the world be secured for the new republic, but the life of the people was virtually the same under whatever rule. When the Spanish joined the Americans and the French against the British, they took the English posts on the river; Fort Bute at Bayou Manshac, the southernmost station belonging to England; Baton Rouge; and Fort Panmure, the site of Natchez.

Beneath the outward show of history — the jealousies of the European state system at work in America, wars, treaties, proclamations — a mighty army was forming, an army that was to possess the heart of a continent not by virtue of a quaint ceremony but by subduing the wilderness and peopling it with their children and their children's children, an army beyond the petty authority of law and convention, an army lawless and wild and free, yet moving steadily westward in inexorable conquest. History falters before this migration. It cannot be "explained," it cannot be put down to any of the simple motives that might comfort the explainer. There was still land, and good land, on the eastern slope of the Alleghenies. Yet this army marched on as though the gates of a new Eden had been flung open and man in his innocence freed again to gather the fruits of the earth.

2

The Invasion

Word of the fertility of the western country went all through the East, acquiring a legendary quality, as of a land flowing with milk and honey, bearing all the riches of earth in overwhelming abundance. The advance guard was already there. Stray wanderers with a thirst for solitude had long since made a way through the wilderness. After 1763 the British outposts had attracted adventurous souls. The Ohio Company had established numerous settlers. Daniel Boone had led a company into Kentucky.

Emigrants from the United States formed a settlement in the country of the Illinois as early as 1781. James Moor, so the record reads, came with his family, accompanied by James Garrison, Robert Kidd, Shadrach Bond, and Larken Rutherford, out "through the wilderness from Virginia to the Ohio, then down that stream to the Mississippi, and up the latter to Kaskaskia."

The invaders came for the most part by water. The Mississippi system was free; an endless flow of life from the far corners of the north and east had begun to pass along it to the heart of the continent, by all the devious, small streams to the great artery that lay at the center of the valley.

The Monongahela and the Allegheny bore the earliest settlers, from the remote forests of northern New York and the stony slopes of the Appalachians, toward a warmer, richer earth. Flowing together at Pittsburgh, the two rivers formed the Ohio, which was broad and deep. The *Pennsylvania Journal* in 1788

advertised boats for sale at "Elizabeth-Town" on the Monongahela. They were "Kentucky boats," of different dimensions and
sizes, to be had at prices as low as any on those waters. To prevent the detention of travelers to the West, which was all too frequent because of the scarcity of boats, the proprietor had erected
a yard on the premises "where timber is plenty and four of the
best Boat Builders from Philadelphia are constantly employed."

There was no adventure that could be compared to it, none
that so stirred the imagination as leaving behind all that was
known and familiar and striking out on a primitive road for a
point at the headwaters of the nearest navigable stream. It was
the young who were naturally attracted to this kind of voyage. A
man married with enough money in his pocket for the cost of the
journey, and man and wife struck out from the settled farming
country of New England or New York State for the unknown, a
destination lurid with the colors of myth and legend; and forever,
for years, decades, a lifetime, the leavetaking desolate with that
sense. An agent, friend, relative had sent back word of land
available, a site for clearing. But this knowledge was uncom-
firmed by any familiar geography. They were bound for Darien,
for fabled country.

The young adventurers had a tedious way to go before they
reached the river. They walked along beside their load, which
contained indispensable furniture, a gun, seed and supplies, a
Bible, or heirloom. Nights they stopped at taverns, buying supper and breakfast; they would make a hasty dinner beside a convenient spring. Their meager store of money melted away and
they were driven to those sharp practices which earned them
such a bad name with a generation of tavern keepers. In his turn
the innkeeper had a store of tricks to catch the unwary. Which
came first, the adventurer's egg of sharpness or the chicken of the
tavern keeper's meanness, it is impossible to say. It depended on
who told the tale, and there were tales aplenty, of fabulous
sharpness, fantastic meanness. It took all a man's shrewdness
and wit to keep a stock of money sufficient to buy a boat, with
some left over for settling on the land.

Arriving at the port where they were to take water, they again had to watch out for tricks, for early boat builders played wickedly upon the innocence of landsmen. They sold these eager immigrants tubs made of worm-eaten timber and unsound plank, craft so poorly and hastily caulked that they would spring a hundred leaks when they had been in the river only a few hours. "But this danger is now so well understood, that few immigrants purchase, until they have had the inspection of some person qualified to judge." A true Yankee would build his own Kentucky flatboat with his own tools. There were so many skilled builders — every other person was in the boat-building trade at Pittsburgh — that the price remained low enough. When the spring rise was on, it was fatal to wait. A brief delay risked weeks of waiting or disaster in shoal waters.

Many and flourishing were the kinds of catastrophe that lay in store for the green newcomers. Indians used hellish devices to lure passing boats to the shore. White captives were compelled to stand on the bank and plead to be rescued. Through a screen of branches and flickering light, red faces painted white were convincing enough. And at every narrow bend the Indians might be waiting to swarm out from overhanging trees.

Far worse were the white outlaws of Cave-in-Rock — the terrible Harpe brothers, Murrel and his gang, and Mason and Stewart. Theirs was an avaricious cruelty, passionless and perverse. By cunning or sheer force of numbers they overwhelmed boatloads of immigrants, robbed them, held them prisoner, tortured them, and finished by slitting the bodies and stuffing them with stones so that they would sink in the river. The Harpes were kill-crazy, murdering for the sheer wanton pleasure of it, and the other inland pirates were not much better. They infested the trails and the traces as well as the river, and how many their victims and how great their loot one may only surmise. These men were, like the weather, or a stage of the river, a natural hazard that one encountered on the voyage to Darien.

When the day was fine — the soft, blue green of spring, or the keen, stirring air of fall — a trip down the Ohio was one to rouse the faintest heart: the sudden glory of morning, with the broad water painted in thin, gold ripples; the slow, melancholy beauty

of dusk, as night drew down and those in the boat gained from
their human nearness and aloneness together a sense of calm se-
curity.

As was common then, several families have joined together to
fit out a large boat. They have sold their horses; the wagon, disjointed, is on the roof of the crude cabin. A copy of *The Ohio and
Mississippe Navigator* tells them all they need to know about the
channel and the shoals; on each page of the book is a detailed
section of the river, with here a sandbar and there an eddy. The
men study these charts with grave care and not infrequent disputes.

There is a fiddle on board. In the broad stretches where the
boat steers itself, the fiddler sets up a lively tune. Whiskey is
cheap and plentiful and strong enough to keep off the chills. The
women potter over the open fire, built on a base of clay, talking
their women's talk. Tow-headed brats — the chief crop of the
early years — run all over the boat. Laundry flaps in the wind.
So, like an army with banners, the invaders passed down the
Ohio, a narrow line that advanced with the force of a glacier
even farther into the great valley.

To Indiana from the boatable heads of the Ohio it was seven
or eight hundred miles by the devious course of the river. To the
junction of the Ohio and the Mississippi was more than a thousand miles. A distinction was made in the early period between a
"Kentucky boat" and a "New Orleans boat"; the latter was heav-
ier and stronger because it had a harder and longer journey to
make. When the destination was Illinois or Missouri, above the
mouth of the Ohio, it was considered advisable to exchange the
unwieldy Kentucky flatboat for a keelboat. But this was much
later. Early immigrants were prepared to stop in Ohio or Indiana. Because of the scarcity of sawed lumber far down the river,
the boat grew in value as it floated on. The first schoolhouse in
Cincinnati was made out of the lumber from a flatboat. When
they arrived at their destination, a family would knock their boat
down and use the planks to build a crude shelter.

Thus did the first comers add houses to lands and begin the
new life. These were sons of toil. The gentry from the South

came across country, passing like the children of Abraham into
the promised land, with their flocks and their herds, their maid-
servants and their manservants. But they, too, sought land along
navigable streams; they needed waterways to carry their produce
to market. They settled first in Mississippi and western Tennessee, later in Missouri and the southern part of Illinois.

For a number of days in a row at least a hundred settlers a day,
most of them in caravans of Biblical fullness, passed through the
village of Saint Charles on the Missouri, not far from the junction of that river with the Mississippi. Timothy Flint, a Presbyterian minister from Boston who had set out on the river route to
evangelize the migrants could see — his report of his journey and
the narrow escapes from death of his family and himself was
widely read — from the cliffs near the town, over the broad
plain, to the ferry where the travelers crossed the Mississippi. In
one train there were nine wagons, each harnessed with from four
to six horses. They were traveling with at least a hundred cattle,
as well as the numbers of hogs, horses, and sheep belonging to
each wagon and tended by four to twenty slaves. "The whole appearance of the train, the cattle with their hundred bells; the ne-
groes with delight in their countenances, for their labours are
suspended and their imaginations excited; the wagons, often carrying two or three tons, so loaded that the mistress and children
are strolling carelessly along, in a gait which enables them to
keep up with the slow travelling carriage; the whole group occu-
pies three quarters of a mile.... It is to be a very pleasing and
patriarchal scene."

Whether they came by road or by water, with the fullness of
the prophets or only the clothes that covered their nakedness,
they soon had produce to market. It is amazing to realize how
quickly trade sprang up along the whole system of rivers draining into the Mississippi. As early as 1763, when Spain acquired
Louisiana, $80,000 worth of deerskins and $4000 worth of tallow
came down from the up-country to New Orleans. The increase
under the Spanish was very rapid. Soon the trade in furs alone
amounted to $100,000 at New Orleans; lumber was being
shipped down the river in large quantities for the Cuban sugar

trade. By 1785 several Philadelphia merchants had found it worth their while to establish agents in New Orleans to deal in the produce that was floated down the river system. The only other method of shipping to the cities on the eastern seaboard was by Conestoga wagon train across the Alleghenies, and the freight rates by this route were all but prohibitive.

The exports of the Ohio country were valued at $975,000 in 1798, and they were increasing by about $300,000 annually. In 1802 the shipments from Kentucky alone amounted to $1,182,-864, and from the Ohio and Mississippi valleys about Bayou Manchac the value of exports was $2,637,564. An irresistible tide, which was to swell to the proportions of a flood, had begun to pour down the great river. Here, from Cramer's *The Navigator* for 1811, is what this tide bore from November 24, 1810 to January 24, 1811, in 197 flatboats and fourteen keelboats that passed the falls of the Ohio: 18,611 barrels of flour, 2,373 barrels of whiskey, 3,759 barrels of apples, 1,085 barrels of cider, 323 barrels of peach brandy, 15,216 pounds of butter, 64,750 pounds of lard, 6,300 pounds of beef, 300 pounds of feathers, 114,000 pounds of rope yarn, 681,000 pounds of pork in bulk, 20,000 pounds of bale rope, 27,700 yards of bagging, 817 hams of venison, 4,608 hams of bacon, 14,390 tame fowls, 155 horses, 286 slaves.

And in exchange, during about the same period, there came twelve barges and seven keelboats freighted with this cargo: 813 bales of cotton, 26 barrels and kegs of fish, 28 cases of wine, 1 bag and 1 barrel of allspice, 1 demijohn and 1 barrel of lime juice, 1 bale of bearskins, 28 boxes of steel, 438 hogsheads of sugar, 1,267 barrels of sugar, 1 barrel of fish oil, 2 bags of pepper, 28 bales of wool, 21 bales of hides, 453 bales of hides (dry), 1 barrel of rice, 5 barrels of molasses, 128 barrels of coffee, 29 barrels of indigo, 6 tons of logwood, 18,000 pounds of pig copper, 1 box of crockery.

The new invaders were not content to till a little land and eke out a frugal life with the trade in furs, as the French petite bourgeoisie had been. Nor were they willing to placate the Indians. In their impatience, their arrogance, they were prepared to sweep every obstacle aside. If the Indians stood in their way, so did the Spanish, who were in possession of Louisiana and the port of New Orleans. Spain was soon made aware of the strange new force that had come into being in the wilderness. Vast and empty as the country still was, there was a growing apprehension in New Orleans that the people who were pushing into the new country to the north would respect neither laws nor limits.

Europe had reports of this peculiar phenomenon, this remarkable migration of a free people, and yet failed utterly to comprehend its significance. The wars that the European powers had waged almost constantly for more than two generations were about to culminate in the Napoleonic debacle. The rulers of Europe were so engrossed in the state system, with its insane jealousies, its inevitable struggle for supremacy, that they could hardly have been expected to understand what had happened in the remote valley of the Mississippi. It was something new in the world, this tide of humanity floating down the rivers of an unpeopled continent. Yet Europe could only ponder on ways and means of turning the tide to some secret purpose within the state system.

For more than twelve years after the peace between the United States and Great Britain in 1782 Spain was to resist the encroachments of the immigrants down the river. The Mississippi was a Spanish canal, or so the governors of Louisiana seemed to feel, and Spain had the right to charge fees for the use of her canal in order to keep off barbarous interlopers who came from over the Alleghenies. Sometimes by formal diplomacy, more often by intrigue and guile, a succession of Spanish governors sought to preserve the province in their care and the river that was the highway of the province. To make the Spaniards' task more difficult, England had agreed with America in a secret treaty to ignore Spain's claims to the eastern shore of the Mississippi.

The right of navigation was at the root of the hostility that slowly took form. The settlers in the western country looked upon the Mississippi River as inalienably theirs; whatever treaties or governments might say, it was the vital heart of their Eden. And so even judicious, discreet General Washington wrote to Jefferson in June of 1785: "The emigration to the waters of the Mississippi is astonishingly great, and chiefly of a description of people who are not very subordinate to the laws and constitution of the State they go from. Whether the prohibition, therefore, of the Spaniards is just or unjust, politic or impolitic, it will be with difficulty that people of this class can be restrained in the enjoyment of natural advantages."

There was smouldering wrath through the western country as word spread that statesman John Jay had yielded, and Congress might do likewise, to the demand of Spain, surrendering the Mississippi for a considerable period of years, perhaps as long as a quarter of a century. Although Spain may have failed to comprehend the significance of the entity — quite beyond the petty dogmas of state — created by the western movement, Spanish diplomats had an insidious knowledge of the surest way to foment disunion. Spain's proposal to Jay laid down the first lines of sectional antagonism in a pattern that has persisted to the present day; a sectional hostility — sometimes as strongly motivated as it was in 1785, or merely an inherited, traditional antagonism — is often the deciding factor in contemporary political and economic quarrels.

What Gardoqui, the Spanish agent, proposed to Jay was a commercial treaty of great advantage to all Atlantic ports in return for the sole right to the great river. This in itself — apart from ancient resentment that had grown out of the continued domination of the parent states, the failure of parent militias to protect settlements from the Indians, the attempt to limit immigration to prescribed areas — would have been enough to inflame the West. It was like proposing to barter away the Island of Manhattan and the harbor at Boston.

Boldly, on August 3, 1786, Jay reported to Congress a plan for shutting off the river for a term of years in return for definite commercial gains. There had never been such a violent issue before the Congress. The South and the West were in one warring camp opposed to the East and the North so long as the freedom of the river was jeopardized. Seven states were for Jay's plan, five against it; the Articles of Confederation required nine states to decide a question so momentous. Meanwhile, as debate raged, the wrath of the West took shape in the threat of an army, twenty thousand strong, to defend the Mississippi.

Angry talk of secession rang through the woods and gave brief hope to two adventurers. James Wilkinson and Aaron Burr sought, like the European powers, to gain a foothold while the government of the new republic remained weak and disjointed. The West was still a prize that glittered in the European mind like a bauble on a Christmas tree. Wilkinson, who seems to have been a man without any honor, set up a traders' capital at New Madrid on the Mississippi and from this vantage point plotted with Estaban Rodriguez Miró, the Spanish governor at New Orleans, to separate the West from the East and to create out of the western territories a puppet state under the domination of Spain. When, a little later, Burr came down the river with another mad scheme for forming a dominion out of Louisiana and the Spanish colonies in the South and West, Wilkinson first deceived and then betrayed his friend.

These plots and intrigues were short-lived. From the bitter disaffection along the river, where it was believed the East would for a price gladly betray the West, the schemers gained a momentary, false hope. Europe was coming to a belated realization of the fact that the wealth of America lay in her enormous potentialities for commerce. France and England were almost as occupied as Spain in trying to regain lost possessions in the Mississippi valley. The shade of La Salle, who had given his life in an effort to convince his country of the wisdom of colonization and trade in the New World, must have enjoyed this spectacle. There were times when the federal government at Washington seemed almost as blind as Europe was to what was happening across the Alleghenies. But at least Jefferson understood. He bought the Mississippi country from Napoleon, thereby ratifying a conquest long since achieved.

It was something strange and marvelous and not a little terrifying that had happened in the wilderness. A wandering people had been given a country of incomparable richness; they were free as man had never been free before. It was a wild, proud, fierce kind of freedom, an arrogant freedom, a headlong, reckless, dancing freedom. And nowhere was it so proud, so wild, as in the men of the river, the men who were half horse and half alligator.

It took men who were superhuman to carry on the commerce of the rivers before the steamboat, men who were half horse and half alligator in their endurance. The downriver trip, by keelboat, was easy enough for these water giants; they had only to keep in the current and, rarely, to push the boat off a sandbar. They were free to drink and play cards and fish and rollick and shoot and sing and dance juba. To the settlers along the river they were a torment and a terror. With the force of a tornado they would roar through a peaceful settlement, drunk and happy, bent on fighting or finding women. Householders barred their doors and walked cautiously down the back streets. Camp meetings were never safe from their assault.

At Natchez-under-the-Hill the keelboatmen had their own fierce little hell. From here on the river was broad and deep, as easy to navigate as an ocean. All the pleasures were to be had at Natchez; they ran out to meet you. One traveler noted that screaming bawdy-tongued women had been known to tear the clothes from a man's back in the street. The shouts and roaring curses, shrilling fiddles and drunken laughter, continued all through the night, the noise so loud sometimes that it came to the ears of respectable Natchez on top of the hill. Visitors describing this Mississippi hell, sprawling sluttishly over its mud flat, thought it only just to say that a few decent men resided there, Yankee traders who had, by the nature of their business, to be close to the river.

The journey upstream was, in bitter contrast, a long, grueling, continuous struggle against the current of the river, relieved only at those rare intervals when the wind was from the right quarter and the sail could be used. It took anywhere from three to four months to go from New Orleans to the trading towns at the head of the Ohio. For each man in the crew there were three thousand pounds of cargo. When the banks were open enough, the crew pulled the boat upstream by a rope called the cordelle, which was fastened to the mast. They all heaved and tugged and strained at this rope, floundering over rocks and through mud and sand, fighting against the undergrowth of young willows and rank weeds. Half horse and half alligator. In shallow water they could pole the boat, which was almost as difficult, and, in rapid water, dangerous in the extreme. Again they bushwhacked; that is, they grabbed branches and young trees on the shore and pulled themselves along — a slow and awkward method. There were oars, three on each side, but the current of the river, with its wild rushing and twisting and turning, made it impossible to use them except in occasional stretches of quiet water.

Ascending rapids was most trying of all. The entire crew was put to it to hold the boat in place while one at a time each man shifted his pole to a place of better vantage. "The slightest error in pushing or steering the boat exposed her to be thrown across the current, and to be brought sideways in contact with rocks would mean her destruction. Or, if she escaped injury, a crew who had let their boat swing in the rapids would have lost caste. A boatman who could not boast that he had never swung or backed in a chute was regarded with contempt, and never trusted with the head pole, the place of honor among keelboatmen."

None but the brave and brawny enlisted in this service. And as they sweated and slaved under the burning sun, stripped to the waist, they acquired a phenomenal toughness. At night they swallowed their rations of whiskey, half-burned meat and half-baked bread, and then flopped down on the deck to sleep. They thrived on such fare. Their cockiness, their lustiness, their gluttony were known throughout the West. The king of these men was Mike Fink, a hero, like Daniel Boone and Davy Crockett, who could outfight, outswear, outrun, outshoot, outdance, outsing all of his kind. Mike had begun life in Pittsburgh when it was little more than a fort and had risen while still a stripling to eloquent kingship of the western waters. Hear his war cry, his official challenge, delivered in a stentorian roar while he beat his chest and kicked his heels like a young stallion:

> I'm a Salt River roarer! I'm a ring-tailed squealer! I'm a reg'lar screamer from the ol' Massassip! WHOOP! I'm the very infant that refused his milk before its eyes were open, and called out for a bottle of old rye! I love the women an' I'm chockful o' fight! I'm half wild horse and half cock-eyed alligator and the rest o' me is crooked snags an' red-hot snappin' turkle. I can hit like fourth-proof lightnin' an every lick I make in the woods lets in an acre of sunshine. I can out-run, out-jump, out-shoot, out-brag, out-drink, an' out-fight, rough-an'- tumble, no holts barred, ary man on both sides the river from Pittsburgh to New Orleans an' back ag'in to St. Louiee. Come on, you flatters, you bargers, you milk-white mechanics, an' see how tough I am to chaw! I ain't had a fight for two days an' I'm spilein' for exercise. Cocke-a-doodle-doo!

Dressed in scarlet shirts and bright blue jackets, the boatmen were lords of creation. Inevitably the French felt the impact of these invaders. The character of Saint Louis was altered by the indomitable boatmen. One tall tale of Mike Fink describes his response to the politesse of the French as it existed on the banks of the Mississippi. A few of the keelboatmen were invited to a dance at Madame Tisan's, where there was some "awful polly-vooin' and French fashions, you know, but gals was mighty peart lookin', as French gals aways is, and it was 'Wooly voo dance, Miss?' and 'Wee, Munsheer!' and dosey-do, and shassey, and toe-nail, and break-down, I tell you, jest as if we'd been all acquainted all along." But during the course of the evening a quarrel occurred and Mike, to get revenge, dropped a couple of pups into the huge kettle of syrup that was boiling over the fireplace. This was not discovered until the syrup was served on pancakes at the end of the evening.

Remotely, where the mounting stream of trade and travel passed by without pause, vestiges of the French culture survived intact, like curious shells cast upon an alien shore. At Kaskaskia

and Sainte Genevieve the small world of the French petite bourgeoisie was hardly disturbed. There is an occasional glimpse of
amenities pleasantly observed, a gentle obbligato lost in the
roaring chorus that the oncoming army sang. One sees the gentry
of Kaskaskia returning from a ball in Sainte Genevieve. It is
early morning; the smokelike mist is lifting from the river; the
voices of the slaves who row the barge are raised in song, deep
and low over the broad water, in farewell, oh farewell to the
party on the bank. This glimpse and then the scene quickly
dwindles. Kaskaskia was to shrink to nothing; the Mississippi
was to carry away the last stick of it with the crumbling earth of
the mud flat on which it was built.

3

In the Year of the Comet

Before the Mississippi could come into its own a miracle had to happen. A boat that would move upstream against the powerful current of western rivers was regarded by river men of the time as still in the realm of the miraculous, the fantastic. It came in a year crowded with miracles, filled with the amazing and the extraordinary, a year when the stars were crossed and nature was out of joint.

The spring of the year 1811 began with a devastating flood. The memory of the earliest settler went back nearly a century to recall anything that equaled it. Bank-full, the Mississippi became a vast inland sea, marked here and there by fringes of half-submerged trees. New Orleans felt the dire effects of the floodwaters and dreaded the fevers and pestilence that were sure to follow. Along both banks the bottomland, so rich for cotton and sugarcane, was long under water. Crops were destroyed and it was impossible to make a second planting. Villages such as Kaskaskia and Sainte Genevieve knew a sharp want of food. When at last the waters receded, swamps and steamy dampness were left behind. The whole valley shook with ague, a plague of chills and fever.

A spirit of change and recklessness seemed to pervade the very dwellers of the forest, one traveler wrote in his journal. A countless multitude of squirrels, obeying some great, unknown impulse left their ancient places of retreat in the North and were seen to press forward by tens of thousands in a deep and solid phalanx to the South. No obstacles seemed to check their extraordinary and concerted movement. The word had been given them to go forth and they obeyed it, though multitudes were lost in the broad Ohio which lay in their path.

In the fall a comet blazed across the sky, a comet of exceeding brilliance and long duration. There had long been a prediction in upper Louisiana that "astonishing and miraculous heavenly appearances" would be seen at about this time, and the comet fulfilled that prophecy. With the unprecedented flood, this was enough to spread profound fears that these portents must foreshadow some awful doom, some immediate catastrophe.

Hardly had the comet faded out, the strange twilight it had created over the forest dimming from night to night, when there occurred the first of the New Madrid earthquakes. A pall darkened the air, the smell of sulphur was strong, geysers of steam and hot water shot up thirty feet high, hell's mouth gaped. In the river it was as though some huge leviathan lashed its tail in torment. A barrier was thrown up in the course of the tremendous upheaval, and for a time the current swerved sharply. (Contemporary records say that the Mississippi flowed, briefly, to the north instead of the south.)

While these extraordinary events had been occurring in the West, there had been in preparation in the East the steamboat, the man-made miracle that was to change the whole tempo of western life. Chancellor Robert R. Livingston and his associates had laid most careful plans to extend their steamboat monopoly throughout the system of western rivers. Livingston was a man of no little shrewdness and force. Born into a position of money and influence in New York City, he had been given the best education the times afforded and launched on a public career. For Jefferson he negotiated, and with great skill, the purchase of Louisiana.

It has been suggested that even then, when he was in Paris as ambassador to France, he was fully aware of the fortune that an individual, or group of individuals, might realize through the operation of steamboats on the rivers of America. To operate in the West, the center of river transportation, it was essential that New

Orleans be in the possession of the United States. A realization of this may very well have spurred the American agent on to the keenest diplomatic effort.

While in France, Livingston spent considerable time experimenting with steam navigation in a kind of partnership with the inventor Robert Fulton, who had come to Paris following a period of study and experiment in England. They launched a boat on the Seine that was only partly successful. Having failed to interest either the French or the English ministries in his military torpedo, Fulton returned to America and, with funds supplied by Livingston, built the steam-propelled *Clermont* and took it up the Hudson from New York to Albany.

With this achievement Livingston and Fulton sought in the eastern states and in Washington a series of patents and charters that would give them exclusive right to carry on steam navigation for a certain period of years, varying, with the nature of the patent or charter possible under the laws of the several states, from fourteen to twenty. Successful in several eastern states, they began at once to realize a handsome profit from their boats.

One reason, of course, that state legislatures proved so amenable was the fact that navigation by steam still appeared impractical and visionary. "A very sensible member" of the New York legislature said that Livingston might have had a charter for any number of years since the steamboat appeared about as likely a mode of travel as the reindeer in Chancellor Livingston's park. What Livingston and Fulton requested was the most thorough-going monopoly, and when they turned to the West, there was considerable realization of just what that monopoly meant. Only Louisiana, where William Claiborne had been named governor of the territory and had remained to become the first elected governor, granted the eastern capitalists a monopoly charter. But the exclusive privilege of the port of New Orleans meant control of the commerce of the West. Plans were immediately begun for an extension of steam navigation to the Mississippi system.

It was at this time that Nicholas Roosevelt became associated with Fulton and Livingston. Roosevelt was of Livingston's class, also a New York patrician, whose family had been solidly established in America for more than a century and a half and owned considerable blocks of property from which the various branches received a substantial income. They were proprietors then, as they are now, of various comfortable country seats in the neighborhood of Poughkeepsie and Skeneateles.

Nicholas Roosevelt, too, had been experimenting with steam as applied to boats, and he is credited with important original modifications of the early steamboat. His wife had been, before her marriage, Lydia Latrobe, daughter of Benjamin H. Latrobe, a distinguished engineer and architect who had designed the capitol at Washington and many other public buildings. Nicholas decided to make an exploratory trip down the Mississippi in order to map out the flow of the current. And contrary to the sternest conventions of the time, his bride announced that she would make this adventure with him. Here is an important precedent that has hitherto been overlooked: Roosevelts, male and female, off on a perilous journey down a little-known river, with indomitable energy and a casual kind of courage. They made the trip, as one would have expected since they were Roosevelts, a charming, Swiss-Family-Robinson expedition. This quality is in Mrs. Roosevelt's letters:

> The journey on the flat-boat commenced at Pittsburgh, where Mr. Roosevelt had it built; a huge box containing a comfortable bedroom, dining-room, pantry, and a room in front for the crew, with a fireplace where the cooking was done. The top of the boat was flat, with seats and an awning. We had on board a pilot, three hands and a man cook. We always stopped at night, lashing the boat to the shore. The row boat was a large one, in which Mr. Roosevelt went out constantly with two or three of the men to ascertain the rapidity of the ripples or current. It was in this row boat we went from Natchez to New Orleans with the same crew.

The journey, particularly after the party had taken to the open boat, was not without severe hardships, or at least what seemed to these well-bred easterners to be hardships. Roosevelt returned to report to Livingston that his survey showed it would be prac-

tical to take a steamboat down the Mississippi. So, in a yard at
Pittsburgh, work was begun. Men were sent into the forest to obtain the ribs, knees, and beams; these were transported to the
Monongahela and rafted to the shipyard. The shipbuilders and
mechanics had to be brought from New York.

In September the *New Orleans* made her first trial runs. That
Nicholas had taken his young bride down the Mississippi in a
flatboat had been the cause of some pretty lively gossip among
the Hudson Valley set. That now she proposed to go with him on
this crazy steam contraption brought forth open protest from all
the members of the Roosevelt clan and their friends. It was utter
folly, absolute madness, they said. Let him risk his neck if he
wanted to, but he had no right to take this innocent young
woman to what was almost certain to be her doom. The innocent
young woman calmly said that she preferred to go. And she
went.

The *New Orleans* drew wild acclaim everywhere she stopped.
At Louisville she arrived in the middle of the night. Some
thought the sound of her escaping steam was caused by the
comet having fallen into the river. Here, as elsewhere, skeptics
doubted that she could run upstream. A number of guests were
invited on board and while they were still seated at dinner, the
New Orleans backed away from the landing and moved against
the current, to the amazement of the diners.

Coming out of the mouth of the Ohio into the Mississippi, the
pilot discovered the channel, which Nicholas had charted with
such care in his rowboat, entirely changed by the earthquake.
Forced to steer without any marks, it was only by great good
fortune that the boat escaped disaster. At New Madrid the Roosevelts saw the full effects of the earthquake.

The town, a huddle of cabins of clay and logs, was in ruins.
But more frightful was the appearance of the land itself. The
earth during the quake had undulated in waves of a few feet in
height, and these swells had burst, throwing into the air quantities of water, sand, and a kind of charcoal, and leaving long fis-
sures that ran north and south in parallel lines for many miles.
Three distinct shocks, the last two separated by several days, had

wracked the prairie until it bore no resemblance to an earthly landscape.

Although many of the natives were as terrified of the *New Orleans* as they had been of the earthquake itself, others begged Roosevelt to save them. They had been in panic since the first shock, convinced that judgment day was at hand. *"Sauve qui peut!"* was the general cry as they fled terror-stricken. Flocks, herds, and household effects left behind were plundered by adventurers who carried their loot south on barges.

All down the river Captain Roosevelt was to find the face of the country changed. While not more than three or four residents were known to have been killed at New Madrid and Little Prairie, the two principal settlements in the earthquake zone, overturned canoes were reported from time to time. Island No. 94 was altogether destroyed and with it, according to Colonel Sarpy of Saint Louis, a band of river pirates. The Colonel, bound upstream from New Orleans, had put in at Island No. 94 for the night, had in some way been warned of the presence of the pirates and had stayed below. In the morning, when the dark mist that accompanied the quake had lifted, there was not a trace of the island to be seen.

There were many freaks. In a bend of the river ten miles below Little Prairie, a settler had a house with a well and a smokehouse some distance away. When his wife started to go for a pail of water the morning after the earthquake, she could find neither the well nor the smokehouse. They were on the opposite side of the Mississippi. The quake had caused a fissure, and the river had thus found a new channel, cutting the bend in two.

Arriving in the broad reaches of the lower river, the *New Orleans* at last left the ruins of the quake behind. At Natchez the engine failed for a time, and the thousands gathered on the shore thought at first that she would not be able to make the landing against the current. Here the reception of the boat was typical. From the backcountry for miles about, men, women, and children had come by the hundreds to see this wonderful thing. They were permitted to go on board in a long file and the captain demonstrated the mysterious works. "The stewing, sizzling, pheezing, whizzing" engine entranced them. And when the captain blew off steam, they jumped like startled animals, certain that the boat had burst her boilers. Departing, the plucky little *New Orleans* had great difficulty in rounding out into the stiff current but at last she made it and, standing out in the stream, fired a salute which was answered by the huzzas of the people crowded onto the levee, waving flags and handkerchiefs. So she went on her way to her namesake city, where she arrived on January 12, 1812.

It was a thrilling, heroic journey, this first trip of a boat propelled by steam on western waters. But as people along the river well knew, the *New Orleans* had not entirely demonstrated that steam navigation was practical on the Mississippi system. She would endure for a few years in the New Orleans-Natchez trade, in that stretch of broad, easy river, but against the wilder twistings and rushings and buffetings of the untamed Mississippi she would be of little avail. She was not a steamboat at all, as a matter of strict definition, but a ship of the oceangoing type that her builders had tried to adapt to the needs of the river and the necessity of steam.

It remained, as Garnett Eskew has shown in *The Pageant of the Packets,* for a western river man to devise the true steamboat and, at the same time, to break the Livingston-Fulton monopoly. Captain Henry M. Shreve was typical of the strong men the river had made. As a boy, he had been drawn into the procession that passed along the Ohio. He had risen, while still comparatively young, to the rank of keelboat captain, owning and operating a fleet of boats that brought quantities of lead from the Galena district. Through his early interest in steam navigation, Captain Shreve came to know Daniel French, who had established at Brownsville, Pennsylvania the Monongahela Steam Navigation Company to exploit his own type of engine, one with oscillating cylinders. Forming a partnership with French, Captain Shreve took out the second boat built by the company, the *Enterprise,* of forty-five tons register.

In less than two weeks Captain Shreve reached New Orleans only to discover that the Livingston-Fulton monopoly was not the most serious threat to the freedom of the Mississippi. The city was beleaguered; the British army was reported hourly at the gates. Terrified townsmen begged Shreve to carry them to safety. But General Andrew Jackson pressed the *Enterprise* into service for the transport of troops and supplies, a service which Shreve gladly gave.

The wild men of Kentucky and Tennessee had come down from the Ohio in answer to the war cry of General Jackson. "A simple invitation is given," he had written from the Hermitage in March of 1812, "for 50,000 volunteers. . . . Shall we, who have clamoured for war, now skulk into a corner? . . . Are we the titled slaves of George the Third? the military conscripts of Napoleon? or the frozen peasants of the Russian Czar? No — we are the free born sons of . . . the only republick now existing in the world." That was the clear and unmistakable voice of western America.

At New Orleans they were not reassured, with rumors of the British coming from every direction, by Jackson's presence. To the fastidious Creole eye he lacked the heartening glory a general should bear about his person. "I prepared a splendid breakfast," one Creole lady complained, "and now! I find that my labor is all thrown away upon an old 'Kaintuck' flatboatman, instead of a great general with plumes, epaulettes, long sword and moustache." The men who were half horse and half alligator had little that was martial in their bearing.

Ragged woodsmen dressed in skins and hides, they won a supreme victory against the pick of Wellington's troops. That peace had already been declared mattered little, for they were the sons of the only existing republic in the world, fighting the battle against foreign tyranny. They hung their triumph up for all the world to see and they said with it that America was free and America's rivers were freed. Europe understood at last that this was something new under the sun, something that did not fit into the state system.

Having contributed his part to Jackson's victory, Captain Shreve faced those other invaders who sought to control the Mississippi. Counsel for Livingston seized the *Enterprise* for infringing upon the monopoly rights held under the charter granted by Louisiana. Shreve gave bond for the release of his

outlaw steamboat and thus was begun a legal contest that river
men all up and down the Mississippi system followed with unflagging interest.

Not until May 6, long after the news of the end of the war had
reached New Orleans and after Jackson's Roman brow had been
crowned with laurel, was Captain Shreve able to depart for the
return trip. The *Enterprise* proved a profound disappointment.
Only because the Mississippi and the Ohio were bank-full, with
quiet water in the bayous and cutoffs, was she able to reach
Louisville. And then it was a last-ditch struggle. At the falls at
Louisville a crowd had gathered to see her come in and when it
appeared that the little boat, puffing and straining in every timber, would not make it against the swift current of the rapids, a
number of men volunteered to warp her over. Thus she came, a
little ignominiously into port, but with the distinction, nevertheless, of being the first vessel to come up the rivers under the
power of steam.

Now Captain Shreve set to work to build, after his own design,
a boat that would be able to stem the swift tide of the Mississippi.
What he did in his boatyard at Wheeling on the Ohio was to put
a new kind of engine, a "high-pressure" steam engine, on the
floor of the first deck of what was essentially a keelboat. That is,
it was a boat with a hull only very little rounded and with a slight
keel, patterned after those boats that had been so successful in
breasting the current of the western rivers. On top of the first
deck Captain Shreve put a second deck. There were other modifications, but these were enough to make his boat a monstrosity,
a kind of ludicrous eight-day wonder that raised jeering laughter
from doubters and skeptics.

Although some laughed and many doubted, the hope of western river men was in this strange boat. Livingston and Fulton
had stirred up a storm of slowly gathering resentment that was a
little like the storm that had threatened against the Spanish when
they had taken the Mississippi to be their private river. The next
boat after the *Enterprise* to run afoul of the Livingston-Fulton
claim at New Orleans was the *Dispatch,* also the property of the
Monongahela Steam Navigation Company. While loading with

a cargo of sugar and molasses for the Ohio, she was seized and ordered to leave the waters of Louisiana and never return, upon threat of confiscation. Not being prepared to put up bond, the captain had perforce to leave without a cargo. Following this, the *Constitution* was seized and she also was compelled to leave Louisiana waters.

There were furious meetings of protest at Cincinnati and Louisville. The authorities of Louisiana were denounced in angry terms and there was talk of another army that would march down to New Orleans. Congress was asked immediately to set aside whatever grant had been made to the Fulton-Livingston partnership. And as Henry Shreve completed his boat, the women of Wheeling embroidered a banner to go on the jackstaff. "On the one side the figure of Fame blew a trumpet. On the other was embroidered, 'Our friends shall not take from us what we have wrested from our enemies . . . ' " That was a clear enough pronouncement and the thing to be wondered at was the word "friends." But this may have been only a polite expression for the public gaze. The boat was ready to launch, and Captain Shreve named her the *Washington* for his father's commander.

Captain Shreve took the *Washington* out to certain victory. The forces of the West were behind him. Despite one serious accident, the *Washington* reached New Orleans in excellent time, and there Captain Shreve served notice that he was prepared to defend what he believed to be his inalienable right. Robert Livingston was dead, but a brother, Edward, came on board the *Washington* and announced that he would champion the family claim through the highest court of the land if necessary. It was reported that Captain Shreve was several times offered considerable rewards, even so much as a generous share in the monopoly, if he would see to it that he lost his claim in court. But with a proper scorn he rejected these offers. Even the people of New Orleans and Louisiana were said to be in sympathy with Shreve and out of sympathy with Claiborne.

The contest went to the United States Supreme Court, where in 1819, two years after the first voyage of the *Washington,* the Livingston-Fulton claim in Louisiana was held invalid. This had been forecast by an earlier decision of Chief Justice John Marshall, overruling the grant that New York State had made. There was never again, until the Civil War, any question of the freedom of the rivers. Nor was there any real doubt about the way to build a steamboat, for the *Washington* demonstrated on her return voyage to Louisville that Captain Shreve knew how to beat the treacherous shoals and the narrow chutes of the western waterways. Henceforth, they would all follow his model: a boat of shallow draught, with little or no hold, a "high-pressure" engine placed on the floor of the first deck. There would be additions — fantastic, fanciful, and practical — but they would have as a basis this peculiar kind of craft that came into being to meet the urgent need of the West.

At the yard of "Messrs Latrobe and Livingston" in Pittsburgh two or three other boats like the *New Orleans,* ill-adapted to river navigation, were built. The second of these was the *Vesuvius.* These boats came in for a great deal of scorn and ridicule, part of which sprang from the resentment the keelboatmen felt at the intrusion of steam. The first steamboats stirred in these wild, hardy men a specimen of that stubborn pride that sprouted in so many different and curious ways in the western country. A popular newspaper of the time described it as follows:

> There were some mad wags in those days who ridiculed steamboats and steamboatmen. With their pirogues and skiffs, whenever they got a chance, they would make a pass at them for a race. At last it got to be a question of who could beat, the iron arm or the arm of flesh. A wager was laid of a barrel of whiskey, that the skiff could beat the old Vesuvius upstream. It was a jolly sight to the passengers and the people of the town. The starting place was just below Glasscock's Island and they were to run to Natchez. At the word "go!" they both dashed off; the skiff of course had the inside track. I think there was about as much puffing and tail pulling in that race as any I ever saw. The skiff would cut in and hug the bank as closely as possible. They had it nip and tuck — now the steamer and now the skiff, for a

good way up; at length the skiff struck an eddy while old Vesuvius had to breast the current; this gave skiffy the advantage and away she shot ahead and beat her antagonist by a few lengths. Great was the laughter; uproarious the shout, that went up for the skiff, for she had fairly won the barrel of whiskey. It is barely possible that the little craft with her crew and trophy didn't navigate steadily when they returned. They were so proud of beating the steamboat, they were intoxicated with delight, nothing more, I assure you!

But the iron arm would win, and with it the country filled up even faster than it had before. Between 1810 and 1820 the population of the Valley increased from 1,370,000 to 2,580,000. Certain areas had an even more rapid growth. Missouri more than tripled its population in this decade. Land took on a cash value and land sharpers and land speculators came into existence. The seeds of an inevitable growth had been scattered along the principal rivers of the West. Individuals and isolated events seem small and unimportant beside the stream of humanity that flowed into the Mississippi valley.

4

The Great Highway

Democracy was afloat on the Mississippi. While steamboats multiplied with astonishing rapidity, there survived from out of the past every kind of pioneer boat, and the needs of the hour called many strange new craft into being. Designed with the practicality and resourcefulness of a people intent on the main chance, there were boats that were ludicrous, pathetic, desperate in the great pageant that passed along the Mississippi system.

Settlers still came by "Kentucky flat," keelboat, broadhorn, ark, and an infinite number of variations of these loosely defined forms. There were trading scows stocked with Yankee notions, boats that were fitted out as tinsmith's shops, barges that were floating brothels, "wood flats" to peddle sawed logs to the steamboats, cumbersome rafts of lumber on their way to market, shanty boats bearing shiftless, vagabond families, itinerant evangelists, drifters, exiles, and adventurers of every description.

Although in the year 1821 New Orleans received by the 287 steamboats that docked at the levee cargoes that amounted to 54,120 tons, almost as much — 52,750 tons — came by flatboat, barge, and keelboat. And New Orleans could boast that year that the value of her exports were only slightly less than for the port of New York, which had once taken its supremacy in trade so casually for granted. Although the towns on the Ohio contributed by far the greater part of the produce that came down the river to New Orleans, the exports of Mississippi and Illinois were growing in importance; and with this development Saint Louis was taking a commanding place in the river trade. In comparison with New Orleans, it was an upstart village, still little more than a fur-trading post. But the Yankees had come and the town was extending its commerce in every direction.

The narrow streets that had been hewn out of the forest on the bluff in back of the wharf were crowded with all the figures of the West, every kind and color of people and bastard combinations to an unknown degree — copper skins, white skins burned a raw red by sun and wind, and shining black skins. There were Indians from the Delaware, Sioux from the North, the Knisteneaux from the Great Slave Lake, Mandans from the upper Missouri, Shoshoni and Nez Percé, dark, handsome Seminoles, native Illinois, and strays from other and more distant tribes. The trade in furs drew them all to Saint Louis.

And as for the whites, they, too, came from everywhere — Creoles from Louisiana, Cuba, Mexico, Pensacola, Canada; occasional pure-blooded Spaniards; late émigrés from France who had come to escape one political storm or another. Then there were the half-breeds, quarter-breeds, and eighth-breeds. The fur traders and voyageurs were wild as Pawnees, with the mark of distant solitude stamped upon their shy, grave faces. In the diverse crowd it was always possible to single out the gaunt settlers with harsh, hard-bitten mouths, bound West from every part of the settled world. Blacks, hardly a year from the kraals of Guinea and the Congo coast, had exotic tribal marks cut on their foreheads and gold rings in their ears. Others had stopped long enough in the Antilles to pick up a patois of Spanish or French and bright silk bandanas to tie about their cropped heads. The intrepid boatmen who survived in the keelboat service still dominated this diverse collection of people from out of the wilderness.

It was a hard, ruthless, rushing kind of life, full of uncertainties and dangers, agues, aches, hunger, and intolerable loneliness. The settlers partook in common of these trials and they shared, too, a sanguine, easy hopefulness, the promise of a reward that was as inevitable as the flow of the river.

Many, if not most, of the settlers had come to the booming

new town on the Mississippi with little or no money. They were
without the furnishings required for even ordinary comforts and
decency. Their chief equipment was that vague, bright hope of a
land flowing with milk and honey. Crowded into slums that had
sprung up overnight, they suffered intensely through the damp
winter of the valley. Misery and wretchedness were so common
as to occasion no remark.

It was only suffering, phenomenal suffering, heightened by the
colors of melodrama, that drew the attention of the hurrying,
pushing throng. Here is a "numerous" family from Maine,
crowded into one room of Saint Louis's pioneer slum. The husband and father is dying. In the same bed the wife is sick, and
while the visitor is there the husband dies and yet she does not
speak a word, her lips sealed by stoicism or the extremity of her
own illness. Three children are down with the fever, making shift
on a pile of rags in the corner. They have spent their last cent of
money and their present refuge, this single room, is in the house
of a poor man. The crowd would for a moment pause before this
tragedy, embalm it in the easy sentimentality of the time, and
pass on.

For those who were bent on quick fortune there could be no
long pause. They must follow the swift course of the rivers. In the
harbor at New Madrid the traveler got the best view, in sharp
focus, of the shifting flux of peoples who passed along the great
highway. For New Madrid, on the west bank of the Mississippi
just below the entrance of the Ohio, was a halfway point in the
trade of the river. Here was "an extensive and fine eddy" in
which the boats from the whole valley came to rest momentarily.
From the farthest north and farthest south and farthest west they
came; from the lead mines of the Fever River and the Rock
River; from the falls of the upper Missouri; from boatyards on
the Youghiogheny, the Allegheny, the Monongahela; from Chicago and remote settlements on Lake Michigan; from Tippe-
canoe on the Wabash; from the Saline, the Kanawha, the Tennessee; from the remoter bayous of Louisiana. And because they
had come so far and safely through so many dangers, they enjoyed on the calm eddy of New Madrid a respite of ease and loud

jollity, exchanging news, rumors, tales, jokes; swapping horses, goods, whiskey; marrying and mating, all under the urge of haste. At the height of the spring rise there were often a hundred boats covering several acres in the New Madrid harbor.

A multitude of sounds came up from this temporary town that might exist for an hour or two, or for so long as a night. Horses neighed and trampled. Dogs fought. Fowls of every kind flapped and crowed and screeched in crazy, improvised cages on the tops of broadhorns and arks. Pigs grunted. Children bellowed. Women visited from boat to boat, discovering a sudden kinship in the dangers and difficulties of their recent past, recalling the settled ease of what must have seemed a time remote and forever lost.

Here was the rich fertility of the American earth translated into the terms of commerce. From one quarter came the fragrant breath of the pine logs of southwest New York, the cargo of a half dozen boats that floated together down the Allegheny and the Ohio, bound for New Orleans. From another direction the reek of whiskey and the dry sweet smell of tobacco were heavy, rising from the boats of "Old Kentucky" burdened with hemp, bagging and bale rope as well. From Illinois and Missouri came cattle and horses, corn in bulk and in the ear. Other boats were loaded with potatoes, quantities of dried apples and peaches, and barrels of new apples, which gave off their own peculiar musky smell. The boats from Tennessee were piled high with bales of cotton.

If this floating town adhered through the night, as it ordinarily did, then the good citizens of New Madrid might well expect to defend their persons and their property. The men who owned the boats might be law-abiding and cautious, but there were the hired hands, for many of whom this was a great adventure that came only once a year, breaking a round of unrelieved toil. Riotous outbreaks were frequent. New Madrid prepared for these attacks, and took "strong measures." "The proceedings on both sides were summary and decisive" — thus charitably is cloaked a multitude of broken heads, wounded and even dying boatmen.

Swiftly, at the first crack of dawn, the community broke up.

With a tremendous stir and confusion and shouts of hail and farewell, one boat after another cast off, bound for some point north or south on the Mississippi or up the Ohio. By the time the sun was fully up, the broad sweep of the river was empty, the fleet dispersed, the people in their separate boats gone about their infinitely various ways.

Sometimes out of this brief meeting such strong friendships grew up that boats were lashed together for the balance of the downriver trip. Such a conjoined fleet would float considerably faster, and with barter and trade and all sorts of merriment, the time passed quickly enough in this impromptu neighborhood. Apples, cider, nuts, dried fruit, whiskey and peach brandy were sold at retail. To get from one end of the flotilla to another one had a considerable walk, passing from roof to roof. But such travel arrangements were usually short-lived, ending in a quarrel provoked by one moral storm or another. The final exchange would be a volley of oaths that continued until the opposing camps were out of earshot.

It would not be long, said serious historians, surveying this extraordinary migration, before the inhabitants of the Mississippi valley would be as famous as the Chinese for having their homes on the water. The Mississippi was certain to be a second Yangtze. It was probable that babies would learn to swim before they learned to walk.

On one very large flatboat was a whole town, with a tavern, dry-goods, grocery, and dram shops. The inhabitants of this town, incidentally, spent a great deal of their time taking drams. One floating tinner's shop on the Mississippi employed a considerable number of men; it went from town to town, passing on when there was no more to be done. A floating blacksmith's shop could shoe a dozen teams at once. The retail trading boats that touched the wilderness at a half dozen borders were stocked as elaborately as a prosperous store in an eastern town. It was a boast of the West "that the delicate hands of the vendor would bear comparison with those of the spruce clerk behind our city counters."

There were crazy boats run by lunatic inventors; boats that employed cattle, horse, and man power to run all manner of treadles and paddles. You saw unwieldy pirogues from out of the past, great canoes fashioned from hollowed logs, some of them capable of a load of two or three tons. Spanish and French traders, commonly called "chicken thieves," used a kind of pirogue. It was not uncommon to see voyageurs, their appearance and mode of travel little changed in a century. Escaped slaves, cutthroats, and sharpers of every description were numerous. Near the levee at each town a collection of boats gathered in the spring for nefarious business of one sort or another. These were "floating mansions of iniquity . . . resorts of all kinds of bad company."

This inordinate, this irresistible, this magnificent flow of life was the common experience of nearly every man in the valley. There was hardly a backwoodsman so remote, a merchant or professional man so unenterprising but that he had made at least one trip to New Orleans. It was the most common method of taking produce to market — to build a flatboat and float down to the seaport at the end of the river. The boat was sold for lumber at New Orleans and the owner and his hands took deck passage on a steamboat north. Often farmers formed a partnership to outfit such an expedition. It was work, but it was adventure too. The urge of the river, its insistent, unfailing invitation, was strong. Scarcely a man who did not feel it.

This constant current of travel and trade had a profound effect on the character of the people of the valley. While the float downstream did not require arduous or exhausting labor, it was a journey filled with sudden peril and alarm. There were rapids, eddies, snags, sawyers, sandbars, heaped-up wrecks, islands with their treacherous shoals. A voyage down the Mississippi was considered far more perilous than an Atlantic crossing. Young men were molded by it. They acquired a thirst for change, excitement, adventure in foreign parts. On the other hand, it gave them the sense of belonging to a particular section of the country, a region that they knew and at least partly understood. The river itself

was a common bond that united, however loosely, the rawboned
lads along the Illinois and the Creole dandies who paraded the
streets of New Orleans.

Abraham Lincoln came down the Mississippi with produce as
a young man, first in 1828 and again in 1831. He was typical of
hundreds of thousands who came down the river, saw its strange
sights and strange peoples; shut away in the distant wilderness,
landlocked, and then the experience of the great highway of the
West. It is clear how this experience must have assaulted the
senses and the mind of the shy, diffident-seeming young man
from the Illinois. He saw slaves sold on the auction block in New
Orleans, saw the buyers try the firm flesh of young wenches,
handle them and pinch them as though they were mares or heif-
ers.

New Orleans was the crowning experience for these rustics
from the back country. If Saint Louis was still a raw, beginning
town, New Orleans in 1825 was a city of compact elegance. A
large destiny hovered over it; the nation looked to New Orleans.
In writing to William Claiborne, whom he had appointed the
first Governor of Louisiana Territory, President Jefferson had
said:

> New Orleans will be forever, as it is now, the mighty mart of
> the merchandise brought from more than a thousand rivers,
> unless prevented by some accident in human affairs. This
> rapidly increasing city will, in no distant time, leave the em-
> poria of the Eastern World far behind. With Boston, Balti-
> more, New York and Philadelphia on the left, Mexico on
> the right, Havana in front, and the immense valley of the
> Mississippi in the rear, no such position for the accumula-
> tion and perpetuity of wealth and power ever existed.

So New Orleans believed, and so the East half believed.

To the staring rawbones from Kentucky and Tennessee it was
a wonderful and frightening city, as foreign as any place beyond
Mexique Bay; foreign-looking and foreign-smelling, the streets
all flooded with brilliant light and high, glowing color. The very
buildings in the old city were strange. Here was not the dull and

sombre red of brick, but rough plaster painted white or yellow.

On one side of the principal square was the river, and opposite it, the cathedral. Such a thing these lads from Illinois and Kentucky had never seen. It had four towers and in one tower there were two bells. All around were the figures of the saints in their appropriate dress and with, according to one early traveler's account, "pale, unearthly countenances." Inside it was "almost as still as in the center of a forest"; the thick walls shut out the common noises of the street so that you heard only the rustling voices of women praying in a foreign tongue.

There were two theaters, the French theater and the American theater, which was in the Faubourg Sainte Marie. There were the ships from the sea, strange and wonderful to river men.

And in the very air of New Orleans was the honey-sweet promise of the women who called out from shuttered doorways a subtle promise, a guarded invitation. Not only the West, not only America, but the world knew of the beauty of New Orleans women. There were charming ladies who, in their sheer muslin dresses, served wine on their cool, broad balconies in the late afternoon. And then there were those other women of every degree of commonness. You could even have a quadroon for a little money; not a famous quadroon, not one of those great beauties whose rare graces were described wherever men gathered to talk about such things; a common quadroon, but nevertheless a New Orleans quadroon — dusky, full of laughter and the promise of curious pleasures.

Only the aristocracy were privileged to attend those famous balls that the café au lait mistresses of the gentry gave. Dressed in gowns from Worth in Paris, and with a poise and dignity acquired through foreign study and foreign travel, the quadroon belles themselves made up a kind of aristocracy; they held a court at which gentlemen were required to behave like gentlemen. There were less famous quadroon balls where, for a dollar, a stranger, even a curious rustic from Illinois or Kentucky, might be admitted. Here the men often came masked and in elaborate costume. These ballrooms, too, had their crystal chandeliers and the women wore satin and silk cut in extreme décolleté. Thus did even common whoring wear a strange disguise in this foreign city.

Yankees from Boston, New York, and Philadelphia were beginning to make their influence felt in New Orleans. They opened branches of eastern firms in order to profit from at least a part of New Orleans's ever increasing trade. Above the city proper were growing up the Faubourgs Sainte Marie and Annunciation; below, Marigny, Daunois, and Clouet. Sainte Marie and many other parts of the city were being built in the American style "and have nothing in their appearance, different from an Atlantic town." There was a Presbyterian church. The Episcopal church was small "but neat and light in its structure."

Yet these prim churches, these neat, light structures, must have seemed not a little incongruous. For it was a foreign place, and foreigners coming there from travels in the wilderness were grateful for its amenities, its ladies, the spectacle of the streets and the coffeehouses, crowded with all kinds of humanity. Every vice and every disease might be found in New Orleans — it was the city's boast.

The capital of the Mississippi, it embodied all that had happened on the river from the very beginning. With the development of the steamboat, New Orleans advanced from year to year, almost from month to month, at a rate extraordinary even for America: forty-one thousand inhabitants in 1819, fifty thousand a decade later. Steamboats were bringing their produce to the port of New Orleans from more and more distant regions. Steamboat captains were daring waters where only pirogues and keelboats had gone.

The *Independence* is credited with being the first steamboat to enter the Missouri. In May of 1819 she left Saint Louis, reaching Franklin, opposite Daniel Boone's Boonslick, thirteen days later. To old Daniel Boone and his many sons this was a stirring sight. For so long they had lived alone in the wilderness, digging out salt and taking it by pirogue to Saint Louis. And now this great steamboat had come to their door. According to a newspaper of the day, "She was joyfully met by the inhabitants of Franklin, and saluted by the firing of cannon, which was returned by the

Independence. The grand desideratum, the important fact, is now ascertained that steamboats can safely navigate the Missouri."

In the same year, the *Western Engineer,* which was built on the Monongahela River and is listed as the forty-fourth western steamboat, was outfitted to take out a party of government explorers who were to establish a site for a military post at or near the junction of the Yellowstone and the Missouri. The party was also instructed to discover the point at which the Rocky Mountains were intersected by the forty-ninth degree of latitude, the western boundary between Canada and the United States. One of the officers in charge was Major Thomas Biddle of Philadelphia and Saint Louis, who was subsequently killed in a duel on Saint Louis's notorious Bloody Island. Scientists in various fields were the principal members of the party that passed up the lonely reaches of the Missouri on the *Western Engineer.* In order to awe and impress the Indian tribes they would encounter, a great copper serpent was constructed which ran along the side of the boat and carried the escaped steam to the bow where it was discharged through the fearsome serpent's head. Three other steamboats and nine barges with a detachment of government troops comprised the official fleet.

Four years later the small steamboat *Virginia* went northward from Saint Louis all the way to Fort Snelling near the site of Saint Paul, the first of her kind to make this voyage on the upper Mississippi. There had been, of course, a prosperous trade in lead that employed six steamboats and a number of keelboats to Galena on the Fever River. While the upper Mississippi was still a wilderness, Galena was a considerable town.

This was pioneering. On the lower river the steamboat trade had already risen to such volume that it was now an important part of the commerce of America. Although there were those who complained that the advent of steam had driven a large number of boatmen — some said as many as ten thousand — from the river, others pointed out the obvious fact that in the construction and fueling of the new steamboats thousands gained a livelihood. According to one estimate, the trade of the

western rivers gave direct employment to 16,900 men. "But add-
ing to those who are directly engaged the much larger number
who are indirectly employed in making engines and in furnish-
ing, supplying, loading and discharging boats, the whole number
of persons deriving subsistence from this navigation, in 1832, was
supposed to be ninety thousand." And this was to increase very
rapidly in the years immediately following.

What was more significant, builders in Ohio boatyards were
aware that the pioneer phase of the steamboat was at an end.
Larger cabins and certain amenities that appeared to the West, at
any rate, as almost effete were advertised in the newest boats.
There were social halls; privacy for families was guaranteed in
improved staterooms. And hardly was one boat off the ways before the hull of another was laid down. Between 1820 and 1828
one hundred and eighteen steamboats were built at Cincinnati,
Marietta, Louisville, Bridgeport, Big Bone, Wheeling, and other
Ohio River ports. Their names are a proud kind of poetry: the
Cumberland, the *Jubilee,* the *Columbia,* the *Atalanta,* the *Red
Rover,* the *Velocipede,* the *Reindeer,* the *Nachitoches,* the *Nep-
tune,* the *Plough Boy,* the *Star.*

From the beginning, the West took an intense pride in its
steamboats, boasting of the splendor of their appointments, their
speed, their power. They were the common denominator of
travel. Even the poorest man could find the few dollars — at
times it was as little as two dollars — necessary for deck passage.
Gingerbread ornament and gilded cabins dazzled the eye of the
rustic inlander. But deeper than this was the underlying sense
that the steamboats were a native form of transportation; a
clause in the charter of western independence, of which the system of western rivers was the principal guarantee; a homegrown
product in which everyone from the lowliest deck passenger to
the largest shipper had a vital stake. This was one of the sources
of the sectional pride that is found again and again in almost
every book and newspaper of the period. Out of the swift development of the Mississippi system came a growing sense of dominion.

The focus of the country was to be its geographical center —

the valley of the principal river, flowing as it did at the heart of the continent, with the great mountain ranges on the east and the west. Many people, and not alone in the West, assumed that this was inevitable. It was seriously written at the time that a canal would one day certainly be constructed to drain the products of the Pacific coast into the system of rivers in the Mississippi valley. All trade should converge upon this system. This was not merely an empty sectional boast but the mature reflection of keen, intelligent observers such as Timothy Flint. In his work there is a powerful expression of what was in the minds and hearts of the people of the valley.

"We know our rights," said Timothy Flint,

> and we are able to maintain them. It is only the little minded and puny that allow themselves to indulge in a causeless and fretful jealousy. There must be a real, palpable and continued purpose to undervalue us and curtail our rights and arrest our advancement and prosperity, before we would allow ourselves to remember our great chain of mountains, and our world by itself. . . . When the western country shall have been inhabited as long as Massachusetts and Virginia, what limits can imagination assign to its population and improvement? No one can fail to have foreseen, at this time of the day, that the period is not far distant, when the greater mass of the population of our country will be on this side of the mountains. We would not desire, in anticipation, to vex the question where the centre of our national government will then be?

The people along the river had a large sense of their own importance. The independence, the forthrightness, the cockiness, the pride of the West took many forms. They were different from people in the East, they knew it, they boasted of it.

It was above all on board a western steamboat that the traveler saw every kind and condition of westerner, planters, speculators, merchants, traders. The traveler from the East would feel as though he had reached a country beyond the seas and, if he were not bigoted, he would draw the same pleasureable sense of for-

eignness, of strangeness, from his experience. The dialect was
different, the enunciation was different. The more rapid speech
of the westerner was sprinkled with curious similes and gargan-
tuan curses. There was more earnestness, abruptness, to be seen
in the manner of the westerner. "Although we have so often been
described to this traveller, as backwoods men, gougers, ruffians,
demi-savages, a repulsive mixture, in the slang phrase, of the
'horse and alligator,' we confidently hazard the opinion, that
when a little accustomed to the manners of the better class of
people among us, he will institute a comparison between our
people and his own, not unfavorable to us."

With this pride went an extreme hypersensitiveness. It was
true of the nation as a whole but especially true of the West. Foreign criticism was not to be endured. Captain Basil Hall's book
of travels, which seems mild enough in its strictures, was the occasion for a tornado of indignation. Booksellers refused to carry
it. It was publicly denounced one every hand. Mrs. Trollope's
Domestic Manners of the Americans was the cause of an even
more violent storm of resentment. The Mississippi she found
gloomy and depressing in its vastness and loneliness, so unlike
the English countryside. On the Mississippi steamboats she
found life at a very low level indeed — there was no conversation
at table, the men ate with their knives, they spat incessantly and
indiscriminately. Her reactions were those natural to a prim
English gentlewoman who held what her son Anthony called
"social and communistic ideas."

But Americans made no allowances. In the East the reviews
were disdainful, contemptuous. In the West the book was taken
as a direct insult to all that the West prized, to the great Mississippi and the incomparable valley through which it flowed. The
Illinois Monthly Magazine, in a review that appeared in the issue
for August 1832, expressed what the West felt in twenty pages of
scorn, invective, sarcasm, irony, innuendo, and plain hurt pride.
Not lightly could a stranger cast aspersions on the glory of the
West.

5

Boom

As a natural wonder, the Mississippi ranked second only to Niagara Falls. There were those who put it above Niagara. It was compared with the Alps, as another example of Nature (always capitalized) in a mood of consummate grandeur. European travelers had to see it. They had, in the post-Trollope phase, to feel, if they were describing their travels for the benefit of the European public, transcendent emotions and they had to think sublime thoughts. There were heretics who saw in the river only a colossal sewer bearing to the sea acres of mud and tons of floating debris, but such heresies were expressed with timid apology. One European visitor confessed that it had been necessary for him to stand in revery on the banks of the stream on six different occasions before he had been properly overcome with awe and wonder. "It is too sublime for beauty," was the refuge of an American tourist recording his impressions for the public eye.

The traveler's rhapsody was customarily concluded with a forest of statistics, showing how many thousands of square miles the river and its tributaries drained and how vast a population its valley might sustain. Had not New Orleans become the third city of the United States by 1840? And were there not times when her commerce, by river and by sea, exceeded even that of New York? The Mississippi would be the center of a mighty culture; that was a fixed belief. The very names Memphis and Cairo show what was in men's minds. This was to be another cradle of civilization, another Nile basin. Magnificent monuments, pyramids and temples, would rise along the banks of this mightier Nile.

Meanwhile, as flush times swelled to the overwhelming thunder of a boom, it was every man for himself, ruin and death take the hindmost. While steamboat owners sought from time to time to work out some kind of permanent combination that would be for the advantage of all, they never succeeded. Each boat was out for what it could get, each boat was a law unto itself. There were "steamboat lines" but for the most part they were loosely formed associations that did not long survive internecine strife and jealousy over the use of common wharfboats. The rivalry was not among competing owners alone; the volume of business was so great that there was enough, and more, for even the slower, less desirable boats.

A pilot was as jealous of his professional reputation as a prima donna. If he failed to take his boat from New Orleans to Saint Louis in a certain number of days and hours, it reflected not so much on the boat as to him. Most of the racing at this period was not so much to enhance the prestige of the boat for the sake of publicity in the modern sense, as for the sheer joy of racing — a pride and a joy that the whole crew shared, from the lowliest cabin boy, the meanest knife shiner, to the master of the pilothouse. And the passengers, unless they were timid Europeans or apprehensive easterners who had read too much about western steamboat disasters, were aroused to a pitch of wild enthusiasm by a race, crowding from one side of the boat to the other, shouting and cheering, providing free whiskey for all of the crew who might want it, hurling foul imprecations (and sometimes chairs, fire buckets, axes, and timbers) at the rival boat when it came close enough. The rivalry between individual pilots often grew into deadly hatred. Rival pilots were like gamecocks, ready at all times for a fight or a race that might end in a fight.

Here are two boats that have raced through a long, wide, safe stretch of the river, first one in the lead and then the other until passengers and crew are in a state of delirious excitement. Now the boat in the lead, thinking to gain a great advantage, takes a precarious shortcut through a narrow chute. To the amazement of everyone, the rival boat follows. It is gaining. Now it edges in between the bank and the lead boat, violating a basic federal law. Word spreads among the passengers on the first boat that the two pilots are mortal enemies and that the pilot in the second boat will wreck them both rather than concede defeat in the race to the town at the head of the chute. Passengers bring shotguns from their cabins and stand along the rail menacing the rival pilot, who is so close that it is almost possible to hear what he says in the open pilothouse.

When disaster is only seconds away, at the bottleneck end of the chute, the second boat drops back. But it is only because the defeated pilot knew that he would be shot if he were not killed in the collision. That is the opinion of the passengers on the victorious boat. And while all this was happening the captain of the first boat, who was also part owner, paced the deck in a torment of anxiety, not daring even to implore the kingly figure at the wheel to yield the race. A humble supplication was *lèse majesté;* more than this was treasonable insult. If a captain ventured to give an order, however modestly he phrased it, he might find it carried out with a vengeance, to the destruction of his boat.

What was amazing was not that there were so many disasters but that they were not more numerous, for the Mississippi steamboat was a floating tinderbox that burned, once it had caught fire, almost as swiftly as a heap of straw. In one of the innumerable lawsuits that grew out of the frequent catastrophes, an expert witness testified that he did not think it would take more than fifteen minutes for the upper works of a steamboat to burn down to the water line. True, he was a prejudiced witness, but his testimony was not seriously challenged.

Fire might break out in a great many ways on these floating tinderboxes. Even a slight collision with a snag or another boat served to tip over the cook stoves in the galley or the heating stoves in the main cabin, spilling showers of live coals. Candles and lamps in individual staterooms were a great hazard. A careless or a drunken person might convert a boat in a few minutes into a drifting torch. A variety of things would happen to the works, but most terrible of all, the boilers might, and very often did, explode, blowing off half the superstructure and spreading death in many ways, all of them agonizing.

The engineers and their crews were not noted for efficiency or caution. The machinery under their care was often inferior even of its kind, shoddy and hastily rushed into a crudely built hull in order to realize a quick profit while the boom was at its height. There was little order and less discipline. Deck passengers were packed on board with utter disregard for safety or decency and, drunk, they were often an impediment to the work of the crew. Many boats kept a colossal black at the head of the stairs to the second deck, whose sole duty it was to keep unruly steerage passengers down where they belonged.

When there was an explosion, or the awful cry of fire, inferno, nothing less, broke loose. There was utter panic, the most horrible pandemonium, with the weak and helpless clawing at the strong for a chance at being saved. The hope for any but the toughest and brawniest was very slight. Live steam from the bursted boilers was fatal to all those who breathed it. Within a few minutes the river would be swarming with clutching, screaming figures, many of them helpless against the surge of the current. A steamboat disaster ran the whole gamut of human suffering and misery. Mark Twain's account in *Life on the Mississippi* of the death of his younger brother, Henry, is almost too painful to read. Poor Henry was a victim of the disaster on the *Pennsylvania*. Mark was on a boat that followed only half a day behind. More than a hundred of those who had been burned, Henry among them, were in a makeshift hospital at Memphis. For three days the boy lay wrapped in cotton soaked in cottonseed oil and then, mercifully, he died.

Besides the hazards of fire and explosion, there was the constant threat of snags, great trees embedded in the river so firmly that they would shiver a hull as though it was paper. On pitchy black nights these hidden snags cast hardly a ripple on the surface of the water. There was no warning before the boat crashed and perhaps went careening over. Fire might follow. As early as the five-year period from 1822 to 1827 the property loss was $1,362,500. In 1841 there were forty-nine boats lost on the Mississippi and its tributaries; in 1842, sixty-eight; in 1846, thirty-six. Insurance companies would only insure "the best hulls," and their rates were all but prohibitive, from 12 to 15 percent of the cost of the boat being the annual premium. And then the insurance companies claimed that they lost money. In 1847 an annual total loss of $1,920,000 was indicated. This was computed on a total investment in the steamboats of $16 million. There were said to be the wrecks of more than ninety steamboats in the two hundred miles of river between the mouth of the Missouri and the mouth of the Ohio.

Yet the volume of traffic constantly swelled. In 1839 the number of steamboat arrivals at Saint Louis was 1,476, representing a total of 213,193 tons. Seven years later this had increased to 2,412 boats representing 467,824 tons. Ardent river men who gathered at the numerous river conventions held during these years claimed that the total ascending and descending trade of the Mississippi was nearly as great as the whole export and import trade of the United States.

It was only foreigners, and that word included the more nervous and conservative easterner, who feared the western steamboat. Dickens felt as though he were traveling in a powder mill. The very phrase "high-pressure engine" struck a kind of terror to his heart and he spent several days at Pittsburgh, where he was to take ship, trying to determine which was the safest boat.

Native Americans were hardly aware of the hardships of steamboat travel, hardships that persisted through the 1850s. But to the fastidious, travel by steamboat must have been an ordeal. The *Grey Eagle,* in about 1850 was the "No. 1 Floating Palace" of the Mississippi. The ladies' cabin contained twelve small staterooms partitioned off by curtains. The gentlemen's cabin extended down to the officers' quarters, bar and barbershop, ending in what was called "Social Hall," where the men sat about smoking and chewing.

The berths were narrow shelves. The staterooms were so small that two people could not dress in them at the same time, and the only piece of baggage they could take was a carpet bag, which seems to have been an article of travel devised to torture a generation of travelers. The only light at night, unless one had thought to bring candles, was that which shone over the transom from the corridor where there were swinging whale-oil lamps. A corner shelf with a basin and pitcher, and one chair completed the furnishings of these palatial staterooms. "Of course," went one complaint, "there was always a colored chambermaid, and equally, of course, she frished around and seemed to have very little responsibility — no bells, no means of summoning her from her little nodding naps if she happened to be beyond the sound of one's voice."

Few except the southern planters — who each spring migrated to White Sulphur or, it might be, to the old family home in Kentucky — traveled for pleasure. And for these southern families the journey up the Mississippi by steamboat was only a means to an end. They always took a manservant, who eased somewhat the hardships of the journey. His duties were unending. He was always being sent for things that were required from trunks stacked up near Social Hall. As the food on the floating palaces of the fifties was coarse, badly prepared, and dismally monotonous, one of the chief functions of the servant was, whenever the boat stopped "to wood up," to forage for eggs, chickens, milk, and fresh fruits. Privileged to use the kitchens, these menservants prepared special dishes for their respective families. The dining table was set up for each meal in the gentlemen's cabin, stretched along its utmost length if necessary to accommodate all passengers. There was no second table. The following is from the diary of a traveler:

> I recall with a smile on one occasion a very respectable looking stranger boarded our boat at Helena or some such place. At dinner he reached for a bottle of wine. Cuthbert Bullitt touched the bottle with a fork, saying, "Private wine!" The man, with a bow, withdrew his hand. Presently he reached for a dish of eggs. My father said, "Excuse me, private." There was something else he reached for, I forget what, and another fellow passenger touched the dish and said, "Private." Presently dessert was served and a fine,

large pie happened to be placed in front of the Helena man. He promptly stuck his knife into it. "By gracious! This is a private pie." There was a roar of laughter.

It developed that the stranger was a professional gambler who had employed this method to attract attention to himself.

The women occupied themselves with "fancy work," footstools and bellpulls done on canvas. The men talked endlessly and spat with unflagging zeal. So the long days passed and the journey of a week or ten days came to an end. No one complained seriously if a boat advertised to leave sharply at noon was delayed a day, or two days, to suit the convenience of the captain or the owner. Water for drinking and all other purposes was hauled up from the river in buckets "on the barber side of the boat, while the steward was emptying refuse to the fishes on the pantry side." It was a warm gruel of mud, but then, only women drank water.

There were likely to be violent distractions to break the monotony of the journey. Not all the wild men had vanished. It was only the scrupulous, the exceptional captains who sought to restrain professional gamblers on their boats. The gambling gentry were the toughest of the tough, shrewd men who made thousands and hundreds of thousands of dollars and then let the profits of a season slip through their fingers with large indifference, the indifference of men who have learned that the sucker crop never fails. They were unashamed rapscallions who pretended to only the lesser of the chivalric virtues; they would never, well hardly ever, gamble for a lady's diamonds, even when the gentleman claimed to have got them without undue violence. A successful gambler on the Mississippi had of necessity to be adroit, tactful, a preeminent judge of human nature, a fighter who could defend himself with bare fists, teeth, feet, swords, whips, pistols, or whatever other weapon the exigencies of the moment might demand.

Here is George Devol, the beau ideal of his profession. A massive, thick man, with a square, imperturbable face, his heavy-lidded eyes only half conceal the harsh, brutal cynicism with which he contemplates the spectacle of human greed and folly. He has trimmed the gentlemen in the cabin of the *Grey Eagle* of their cash and now he turns to the deckhands, who have been paid off at the last town. The hand of the gambler is always faster than the eye of the gull who tries and tries again, with the confidence that Mr. Devol has planted in his stout bosom, to pick the card with the baby on it.

Stripped clean of earnings hardly won, these simpler gulls grow sullen and resentful. Devol is standing against the bar. His friend the barkeep gives him a nod and he turns, instantly alert, to confront three deckhands come to take their losses out of his hide. At the first he lunges with his head, said to be made of iron, and bowls him over; he sloughs down another with a fist like a ham, grapples with the third, and ends by tossing him out onto the deck. With the aid of Betsey, his revolver, he cows the mate and a further contingent of hands. When the quarrel has gone to a point of open bloodshed, the captain steps in and resolves a truce that endures until Devol is put ashore. But is is plain how this quarrel must have shattered the stilly peace of the afternoon. Murder was not unheard of, blood was often spilled.

Until very late, the men who kept the wood yards were lawless characters who had in many instances sought out the solitude of a wooding station to escape the consequences of crime committed in the settled East. The traveler who had money on his person went ashore at these crude stations at his own risk. He was advised to stay close to the boat, better still to stay on board while the deckhands were wooding up. A traveler recorded in his journal that the proprietor of one wood yard was reported to have murdered his wife two or three days before. But he added that in the West such accidents must be accepted as a part of the dispensation of nature. And besides, the wife was half Indian, which seemed to make the whole incident unimportant.

The river still swarmed with trading scows and small anomalous boats of infinite variety. Their owners were the avowed enemies of all steamboatmen. It was a fixed practice on these small boats never to carry a light at night. When a great floating palace bore down around a bend upon such craft on a black night, the pilot swung hard on the wheel and the air, so long as the two were in sight of each other, was charged with violent oaths. Steamboatmen said that scow owners sought only an excuse for a lawsuit. When it was too late to avoid a collision, the great paddlewheel would walk over the small boat, shattering it to kindling wood, with the injured and the dying in the wheel's foaming wake.

In the larger cities, Saint Louis and New Orleans, the landing stages drew a population of prostitutes. The river front was lined with bagnios in which harlotry ran the color scale from midnight black to purest white. The price went by color, too. Deckhands enjoyed a black woman for fifty or even twenty-five cents. Other whores, the aristocracy of their profession, did an excellent trade on the fine packets. Virtuous captain-owners, jealous of the reputations of their "family boats," found it difficult or impossible to suppress this traffic. As in the early days, floating brothels cruised from landing to landing — Venus couchant on the wave.

A dull voyage was rare. The first-class packets, with their scrollwork and their gilt and their gaudily painted sides, were packed from stem to stern with pushing, scrambling, violent life. There were sober immigrants with their small hoards of money sewn into undershirts or inner pockets. But even they took on the coloring of their environment and succumbed to the lurid promises of the land speculators, indulging briefly in wild hopes. Towns and town lots, squares and plazas, magnificent avenues, and broad vistas bloomed on lonely prairies and more often than not withered and died before a spadeful of sod was turned.

In the early fifties, particularly in the upper Mississippi valley, which was filling up with new arrivals each day, the advantages of the river system were still stressed. Hear the claims of Bowen's Prairie, set forth in bold, black type:

> A Newly Laid Out Town on the Prairie, of the same name, situated in Jones County.... The Improvements since it has been laid out have been unsurpassed by any Town in Northern Iowa. Situated as it is, between the North and South Forks of the Maquoketa River (a minor tributary

of the Mississippi), and in the center of a high and rolling
Prairie, whose area is fully six miles in extent . . . it is bound
eventually to become one of the finest towns in all the
West . . . . Many Beautiful Residences Occupied by stirring
Mechanics and men of business, many more of which are
wanted.

Town lots in Cairo were sold over and over again when the site
was nothing more than a fever-ridden swamp. An article of faith
among those who believed in the dominance of the river system
was that this location, at the confluence of the Ohio and the Mississippi, must inevitably see the rise of a great city. Remembering
his own considerable losses in Mississippi swamps, Dickens was
moved to melancholy reflection by his view of Cairo from the
vantage of an Ohio River steamer. "A dismal swamp," he said, in
which "wretched wanderers who are tempted hither, droop, and
die, and lay their bones." And it was this that had been "vaunted
in England as a mine of Golden Hope and speculated in, on the
faith of monstrous representations, to many peoples' ruin." Of
Keokuk, Iowa on the upper river, Mark Twain says that during
the year he lived there town lots soared to a price that would still
have been high if the ground had been sodded with greenbacks.
The great cities of this country, said a western editor in 1850,
would ultimately be found in the central region between the
Lakes and the Gulf of Mexico. And there was ample reason to
believe that this would be so. By the census of that year Cincinnati had shown an increase of 150 percent, Louisville of nearly
100 percent, Pittsburgh of more than 300 percent, and Saint
Louis of about 400 percent.

The Treaty of Traverse de Sioux in 1851 opened a large area
west of the Mississippi to settlement. The rush to Minnesota that
followed was compared to the gold rush of '49. Fortunes were
being made — and lost. There were stories, fabulous and yet au-
thentic, about what was happening to land values in Saint Paul.
A few voyageurs and half-breeds had camped on the site and
then, by the magic that is peculiarly American, a city had come
into being. A lot, 100 feet front by 150 feet deep, at the corner of

Third and Robert streets, which had sold in 1850 for $600 brought $24,800 in 1856. And not strangers, but residents of long standing paid this price. In the course of a single year, from 1855 to 1856, the cost of a tract of land two miles from the city advanced from $6,000 to $14,000.

On a lesser scale the same thing was happening all up and down the river. The first railroad touched the banks of the Mississippi at Rock Island in 1854 and the car brought thousands of immigrants who took passage by steamboat for the upper river at this point. In the little town of Hastings, on the west bank of the Mississippi below Saint Paul, town lots sold in the first year and a half for as high as $3,000, and $2,000 was a common price. The same was true in Prescott, Winona, and a score of upper river towns.

With the opening of this new territory along the Mississippi above Saint Louis and on the upper reaches of the Missouri, the speculation in steamboats became more frenzied than ever before. The *War Eagle,* in the Saint Paul trade, cost $20,000 to build. In her first year in service she returned to her owners profits of $44,000. The *City Belle* cost about $11,000 and returned in one year a profit of $30,000. The company to which these boats, in common with many others, belonged returned in 1856 a dividend upon a profit of $100,000, besides building several new boats. With such tales in the air what American could resist speculation?

In the spring of 1856, only one month after the opening of navigation, it was recorded that two hundred steamboats had already put in at the Saint Paul levee. The business carried on at the wharves flourished with all the noise, the confusion and the sweaty turmoil of Pittsburgh or Saint Louis. The river boom was at its height; a deafening crescendo, as of the roar of a thousand steam calliopes on a thousand riverboats. First comers had fallen upon the vast forests of pine along the Saint Croix River, the log rafts in the upper Mississippi were growing larger.

Immigrants to Kansas and farther west booked long in advance every inch of available space in the steamers that left Saint Louis for Saint Joseph. The Missouri was so difficult and pilots who knew it so scarce that they commanded as high as two thousand dollars a month during the season of navigation. In the columns of Saint Louis newspapers boats were advertised daily for Sioux City, Saint Paul, Keokuk, Saint Joseph, Council Bluffs, Peoria, Naples, Pittsburgh, Cairo, New Orleans, Alton, the Tennessee River.

In the Mississippi valley there was an awareness that a new way of life had come into being. It would exist for a brief time with a certain clear identity, a certain distinctness, even a certain wholeness. While to the European it seemed crude, violent, inchoate, it nevertheless, in its integrity and its wholeness, impressed itself upon the mind of a genius. In the work of Mark Twain there is to be found the most complete expression of this American way of life, of the experience of western America.

6

Mark Twain's Mississippi

The Clemens family was from Virginia. As a young man, John Clemens had moved with his widowed mother and his younger brothers and sisters to Kentucky. When he married Jane Lampton, of a family that had fought Indians in early Kentucky, he moved for a time to east Tennessee. But it was inevitable that a man of his temperament should pass on with the vast westward-flowing stream. It is difficult to realize how irresistible the pull of that stream must have been, how irresistible were the forces that sent it rolling on. There was always the great hope. Any man might make himself rich tomorrow or the day after tomorrow; that was a fundamental part of the social heritage. It shone large and bright in John Clemens's life.

From Florida, Missouri several Lampton relatives had written urging John and Jane to come to the newest Eden. Florida was on the frontier of the Mississippi, about fifty miles from the great stream, on the Salt River, a tributary. What was more, as the Lamptons must have pointed out, the Salt was considered a navigable tributary that would of course play an important part in the commerce of the region. Changes had come so fast it was scarcely correct to speak of the river as a frontier in that year of 1835. Each season saw more steamboats at the river ports. Saint Louis was a booming town with a population that had passed the ten thousand mark. The Lamptons could paint the future of Florida in colors of dazzling brightness, although it was then only a collection of about twenty houses.

John and Jane Clemens, their four children and their slave girl Jennie, followed the great thoroughfare of the West when they left Jamestown, Tennessee in the spring of 1835. They went by carriage to Louisville, by boat down the Ohio to its confluence with the Mississippi, thence up the great river to Saint Louis, and for the last stage, overland to Florida, about a hundred miles north. They were figures in a crowd. Often it was difficult to book passage on the boats. Saint Louis was filled to overflowing, so that if you were a stranger you might not find a room nor even so much as a bed.

The Clemenses had not been long in Florida when, on November 30, a fifth child, a son they named Samuel, was born. This weak and pewling infant can hardly have occupied the attention of his father for very long. John Clemens was engaged in vast undertakings toward the realization of those dreams of wealth and power that seem to have absorbed most of his thoughts.

After several ventures had failed, he turned to the exploitation of Salt River. Here, too, he followed an established course. There were a thousand Salt Rivers, each one swollen with the tide of imminent destiny. Railroads, insofar as the West was concerned, were a curious experiment that would doubtless always be limited to a few special purposes. The rivers would have no rival in carrying the commerce of this vast new country to market. Such was the fixed belief of the time. Judge Clemens — he had been elected justice of the peace for a term and had thus acquired for life this familiar southern title — followed the best precedents in undertaking to make Salt River navigable for steamboats.

First he obtained from the Missouri legislature an act of incorporation for the new navigation company of which he was president. Next and far more important, he got up a petition to Congress for an appropriation for a system of locks and dams that would insure the perfect and eternal navigability of Salt River. Here, one may say in passing, is a primary pattern of American behavior — the assumption that government exists, like a kindly father, to enable the individual, and incidentally the community in which he lives, to acquire wealth. Briefly there was

high hope in Florida. A boatyard was established by the navigation company and a small boat was actually built for the carrying
trade. And then Congress, as Congress infrequently does, refused
to grant an appropriation to make the Salt River navigable.
This marked the end of Judge Clemens's hopes in Florida. He
now moved his family to a town on the great river that was already the focus of a considerable trade. Steamboats called there
on a fixed schedule that was more or less closely observed. Florida in 1835 had been full of promise. Hannibal in 1839 was a
tangible accomplishment, a river town with a future that was
limited only by the trade of the river. And this trade was growing
so fast that you could see no end to it.

Hannibal was no longer a frontier town. Elements of the frontier survived, as they survive in certain phases of American life
today, but the town was a settled community, with a government
and a code of law, a fairly distinct social scale with varying standards of behavior, a religion, and even a thin gloss of culture,
which consisted for the most part of tag ends of classical learning
and a dilute, saccharine romanticism, which was chiefly the
province of women. These were the elements that made up the
external structure of the town. It was a poor, threadbare sort of
thing, never able to hold in bounds the powerful forces that
made their influence felt without the sanction of the designated
rulers of the town.

These forces were many and diverse. There was the presence
of the Negro, who constantly infused his own superstitions and
taboos, his own outlook, into the minds of the whites, weakening
the authority of the narrow Calvinism that was the official religion. There was the fundamental drive for money, for position — a constant assault upon the social scale in which every
kind of sharp practice was countenanced on the theory that the
individual must advance himself by any means whatever, that
that was his first duty.

Most powerful of all perhaps was the impact of the wilderness
upon the individual who was for the first time set down in it.
There was scarcely anyone in Hannibal who had not known this,
and, for that matter, though the country round about was being

settled in 1839, there was still wilderness at the dooryard. It is impossible to conceive how this affected the mind of the man or woman from a neat town or settled region of the East; it worked in a thousand ways — through the threat of danger, the decimation of diseases peculiar to a new country (ague, chills, and fever), the rewards and penalties of solitude. On the one hand, there was a sense of unconquerable freedom and infinite possesstion in the abundance of fertile land, forest, game; and on the other, bleakness, inversion approaching madness.

And at Hannibal there was the river, the great, mile-wide Mississippi flowing past the door. It was an avenue of escape and at the same time it joined the town to the great world that the river had created, a world with a special high color of its own, the world of New Orleans, Natchez, Saint Louis, the world of Murrel and Mason and the other outlaws, the world of the wild boatmen, the world of palatial steamboats.

The little town was forever bursting out of the patched-up civilization that had been brought — as a chair or two, bedstead, a piece of silver, a family portrait, a family Bible were brought — from over the mountains; it was forever improvising new and often crude and harsh methods for meeting new situations. This was, in many respects, the typical conflict of the West, although it was often brought to an end by the further emigration of the more adventurous and the more lawless, those remaining behind accepted tamely enough the outward and vitiated forms of old authority.

Along the river this conflict endured, because of the very presence of the river it seems to me, for a sufficient time to enable a special way of life to come into being, a kind of compromise that came out of the conflict between the new and the old. Perhaps one may not examine its outlines too closely, nor set its limits in time too narrowly. But it is discoverable, one may find it.

By a coincidence, the boy Samuel Clemens, possessed of the infinite sensitivity of a genius, came to live at Hannibal at what was perhaps the outset of this loosely defined period. He was to live along the river, with one or two brief interruptions, until the world of the river was shattered; that is, for twenty years, the most formative years of his life. In his most important work there is a magnificent record of that world. Yet the factors that were to bring about its downfall were at work through almost the entire period. But so complete and self-sufficient was this world that the final signal for its destruction, the outbreak of the Civil War, came to Samuel Clemens, as it did to most river men, with the abrupt shock of surprise.

In *Huckleberry Finn, Tom Sawyer,* and to a lesser degree, in *Life on the Mississippi* there is above all else an onslaught against the dead and sterile forms of civilization that had been brought from over the mountains. This, as has been made clear, is Mark Twain's great theme. In part one may put it down to Mark Twain's own rebellion, his own lifelong revolt against all that was narrow and stupid and mean and petty, but in larger part his use of this theme identifies him with his time. It was true that even those duly constituted to carry out the forms of law and order were inclined to put aside the law book or ignore the custom that got in their way.

In *Huckleberry Finn* and *Tom Sawyer* the schoolmaster who was, of course, Mark Twain's Hannibal schoolmaster, bears a resemblance to certain of the schoolmasters in Dickens. His pupils he regards as annoying nuisances, little hellions to whom he accords a savage, vindictive ferocity. His vanity, his hypocrisy, his essential meanness are apparent to the smallest child. But where the schoolmasters in Dickens for the most part triumph over their charges, the schoolmaster in Mark Twain is constantly defeated, forever undone by the wild, untamable spirits he is set to control. His frowsy scraps of Latin, his sickly romanticism are rejected. Only one boy, the "model boy" who is the pariah of the school, accepts his rule. This same rebellion against the authority of the schoolmaster may be seen over and over in the popular literature of the time. It is one of the things that most delighted Mark Twain's early public.

In the department of religion there was the same tendency to break out of bounds. There were numberless superstitions, some of them straight from the Congo, that adults as well as children accepted. Mrs. Clemens covered up her head in terror when she saw a white-gowned figure — little Sam sleepwalking — come into her room after the death of her husband; she was sure it was a ghost. Both whites and blacks resorted to hairballs and witcheries of various kinds. In time of stress, as when a violent thunderstorm raked the sky, the doctrine of hell fire impressed its awful weight; but when the nascent air of the valley was all rich with spring smells under a cloudless sky, Calvinism was cast aside. A dog chasing a pinchbug was a welcome distraction for young and old from the tedious sermon of a summer Sunday. Sometimes the preacher was paid and sometimes he wasn't. The poverty of parsons was a standing joke.

As for the law, it was a mere flimsy target for the impatient arrows of men — and women, too — who could never brook its delay. Mark Twain's biographer has told us how again and again the boy saw violence and bloodshed outside the law. He saw an old man shot down at noonday and carried home to die with a great Bible on his chest. He saw a woman fire from her doorstep at a jeering drunk after she had given him fair warning to move on. He saw runaway slaves in irons, heard them groan in their sorrow and misery. Men were always fighting, scornful of the test of the law. Judge Lynch was on the bench night and day. A mob could form, with deep, ferocious passions, before any individual was aware of what was happening. Sometimes, perhaps, elemental justice was done; more often the passion of the mob spent itself with a vindictive cruelty.

For outlaws of whatever age, rebels of whatever kind, there was the shining invitation of the river. Tom Sawyer, Huck Finn and his old man, Nigger Jim, the Duke of Bilgewater, the Lost Dauphin, the lawless raftsmen, rascals, sharpers, thieves, murderers, vagabonds — all found a refuge on the river. They went by stealth, through remote slough and lost bayou, or they swept down with bold defiance, indifferent to the law of the land.

For young rebels this was a primal world, an innocent world. It is there in Huck Finn's stay on the island, in his marvelous float down the river with Jim, in his description of the stars as he lies on the raft and looks up at them, in the storm that tears at the trees. There is the sense of elemental strength — radiant, kind, and then abruptly cruel and relentless. Appealing very deeply to something that is, or was, at the root of many Americans, and rare in our literature, there is, in particular in *Huckleberry Finn* an appreciation of the solitude of the river. It is the identification of the individual with all that is rich and rare and strangely beautiful in his environment. A Thoreau must seek it, a conscious, exclusive solitude, shutting out the town and all the ways of mankind. For the men of the river, a kind of solitude was a part of everyday life, and as real as any other part.

About midway in *Huckleberry Finn,* just before Huck and Jim meet the Duke and the Dauphin, a long passage occurs in which Huck describes their life on the raft. In this, the most superb poetry, is the essence of what I mean. It is not isolation, it is not desolate loneliness. It is a primal world, shared by a companion, its solitude accentuated by occasional evidence of other life — a light on the far shore, a passing raft with voices coming mysteriously out of the fog, a steamboat very small across the mile-wide river.

In the character of the raftsmen, given in the chapter that was ruled out of *Huckleberry Finn* but was included in *Life on the Mississippi,* one may see the same innocence. No better word occurs. Judged by any arbitrary external standard they were, like the keelboatmen before them, thieving, drunken, boastful rascals who would never hesitate to raid a town or break up a camp meeting. But they were not in general vicious men. It was merely that, like the larger forces of their invironment — the wind, the sun, the river — they were utterly irresponsible. Beyond the discipline of their work — which they regarded not as a discipline but as a trial of strength, prowess, and courage that brought them, incidentally, money for whiskey and women — they were swayed by wild, random impulse.

Mark Twain did not invent the chapter on the raftsmen. It would have been impossible to have invented it. Like every other boy who lived along the Mississippi during this period of seventy-five to a hundred years, young Sam Clemens, for all that his mother might scold and rail, knew those raftsmen. They were wonderful and fascinating heroes who told the most whopping stories and sang the lewdest songs. They were obscene, incredibly foulmouthed, but their obscenity seemed only a part of their great gusto, as natural and as uncontrolled as the wind. This gusto, this tremendous energy, is in the chapter on the raftsmen.

When Huck Finn crawled aboard the big floating lumber raft, hoping to overhear a conversation that would disclose whether they were above or below Cairo, the raftsmen were taking their ease. Only in narrow or difficult stretches of the river were they required to man the great sweeps at each end, by means of which the raft was steered. And what did these men, who might be called upon at any hour of the day or night for prodigious labors in cold rain and burning sun, do during their idle hours? They drank whiskey. They sang interminable songs, in solo and in chorus. They engaged in mock and real fights, uttering boasts, half serious, half humorous, of their superhuman ferocity. They danced the breakdown and patted juba. They played cards and plain loafed, too. But most of the things they did were an outlet for the boundless energy that seemed to possess them.

That this wild torrent of energy was a characteristic of the West, and in particular of the river at this time, there is ample evidence. Not everyone was aware of it. Dickens and Mrs. Trollope saw only weary women, tobacco-spitting men, unkempt children. But they saw it from a European perspective, filtered through a different set of ideas and standards; and today, looking back, we glimpse it through another set of ideas. In journals and letters of the time, even in formal books of travel, there is a sense of this vast sweep of energy, the sense of a beginning world in which all the colors are brighter and fresher than anywhere else. This may be in part the glow of high hope, a sustaining belief in what the new country was destined to become, but that these qualities, as of a new and innocent world in which men were endowed with radiance and power, did exist, at least for the people of that time and place, is plain.

There is striking confirmation of this in the work of a painter of the region and the period, who until very late has been strangely overlooked. George Caleb Bingham of Missouri saw the river and the people of the river as Mark Twain saw them.

His paintings convey the same vitality, the glowing freshness and innocence of *Huckleberry Finn,* almost as though they were made to serve as illustrations for that book.

Bingham did a series of river pictures, several of which were lithographed and widely distributed in the late forties and fifties. In *Fur Traders Descending the Missouri, Raftsmen on the Ohio, A Boatman, Watching the Cargo, The Jolly Flatboatmen, The Jolly Keelboatmen, Raftsmen Playing Cards,* and others Bingham took the central figures from sketches in his notebook, sketches that he had made from close personal observation. When he had earned a measure of economic independence through journeyman portrait painting in Saint Louis and other western towns, he went back to his boyhood home, Franklin, across from Boonslick on the Missouri River, and made a "serious study" of the river men he had known.

In *The Jolly Flatboatmen* series — he did several paintings on this theme — there is an irresistible joy of living. The central figure in the pyramidal design is the dancer who sways with his whole body in joyful abandon. The fiddler is swaying to his own rhythm, and a young boy is beating the time with his knuckles on a pan. Other figures are sprawled about the boat, looking on with lazy, amused indifference. Even in his smaller paintings, such as *Fur Traders Descending the Missouri,* now in the new American wing of the Metropolitan Museum, there is the fresh air of a morning world. In this picture a fur trader and his half-breed son are seated at opposite ends of a pirogue, a long, narrow boat that makes a single dark line on the misted river. In the stern is chained a bear cub, seen only as a black oval. The voyageur, a direct heir of that early past, has far-seeing eyes that pierce the great distances of wilderness and water. He looks out at the observer; behind the two extends a long vista, the subtle, soft air of the great valley like a luminous curtain.

There are journals, letters, diaries from this period that convey the same quality. They are not common, but they are to be found as one finds early glass and lusterware. This prose often has the clarity of outline, the bright, primary colors of Stiegel glass. It was as true of the time and the place as the reports of Mrs. Trol-

lope, Dickens, and other European visitors. There were weary
women, there were bleak towns sunk in the mud of the riverbank, such as the one Mark Twain describes in *Huckleberry
Finn,* there was frustration, there was bitter defeat, there was
early death for the heedless raftsmen, there were the wracking
winters and the long damp chill of spring. But there was, too, the
glory of a beginning world, ecstasy, wild delight. The glow of this
was so rich, so brilliant, that the frustration and the embitterment
of defeat seem only faint shadows sketched in to afford contrast
as in Mark Twain's work.

If the river was a way of escape, it also gave to the people who
lived along it a unifying interest. In *Life on the Mississippi* there is
a stirring description of what happened in Hannibal when the
cry was raised, "S-t-e-a-m-boat a-comin'!" That was twice a day,
when a gaudy packet arrived up from Saint Louis and when another stopped on its way down from Keokuk. Drays clattered
over the levee. The dozing clerks along Water Street woke up.
Small boys came running from all directions. The landing of the
boat and the discharging and taking on of passengers were operations in which the whole town took the kind of pride that a family takes in the achievements of its most brilliant member. You
stood on the levee, gaping at the gilt-and-white boat, realizing
that within a few hours it could take you to "Saint Loooy" as it
had brought these passengers from the metropolis; you were that
close to the great world; this boat made you really a part of it.

Of the boys who flocked to the levee twice a day not a one but
longed to ship aboard a steamboat, even in the humblest capac-
ity, as engineer's helper, or "striker," whose chief duty was to
wipe metal with a piece of oily waste. There was a day when
young Sam Clemens could no longer resist temptation. He
sneaked aboard the Saint Louis packet, his biographer relates,
was discovered by a deckhand and put off at Louisiana, Missouri, where there were relatives to take charge of him.

To the boys on the levee a pilot was head and shoulders over
all other men. "Two months of his wages would pay a preacher's
salary for a year." They hardly dared hope so high. Six of Sam
Clemens's contemporaries were to become pilots, one an engi-

neer, two others "mud clerks," another a steamboat bar-
keeper — all in answer to the urge of the river.

As for young Sam, under the pressure of family necessity perhaps, he turned to the trade of printer. Apprenticed, he received
board and clothes and relieved his harassed family of the responsibility of providing his keep. To go on the river, as apprentice
pilot or apprentice engineer, required a certain backing, at least a
small capital. Board on the boats was free for the cub pilot, but
he had to provide for himself while in port and, of course, he had
to furnish his own clothes. The Clemens family was penniless;
Sam's father had died bankrupt.

Under the direction of the oldest son, Orion, the Clemens's
fortunes grew worse, if that were possible. Orion owned the
Hannibal Journal, and Sam worked for him for wages that were
less than he had earned as an apprentice, since the clothes were
shabbier and the board was slimmer. But family loyalty seems to
have kept him at this task until at last he could endure it no
longer. He went away then, hurt and angry, to Saint Louis, New
York, and Philadelphia. In each place he earned his own living
as a printer and had money left over to send his mother a dollar
occasionally.

After a little more than a year he came back to the river. It
may have been only longing, the homesickness of a boy who was
not yet twenty, that drew him back. It is possible, however, that
the river had for him a somewhat larger meaning. New York and
Philadelphia were curious places, full of strange and marvelous
sights; but the region to which he belonged was the region of the
river, a section with a special, highly colored life of its own, a life
with which he was identified.

At any rate, he did return — to Muscatine, Iowa, briefly, and
then to Keokuk, Iowa, where Orion by then owned another
newspaper. And when he left a second time, with the vague, romantic, absurd idea of taking part in the exploration of the
Amazon River, he found a career on the Mississippi. As he was
to say again and again, it was the most satisfying of the many
careers he followed. One can understand why he felt this.

The world of the river was still intact, still complete. For all that the newspapers and magazines of the region wrote about what the railroads were doing to the trade of the river, it was undoubtedly true that the majority saw no possibility of a break in the independence, the supremacy, of this section. The standards of the region were those created by its needs. That is to say, it was not a province but an independent kingdom, however new and crude and uncouth it might have seemed to strangers.

If any man was its acknowledged king, it was the Mississippi steamboat pilot, for his job filled every need. It was dangerous and therefore heroic. To steer a great boat through the treacherous river with the strength of one's own arms was a definite physical satisfaction. It called for skill and the keenest capacities. To do this in the sight of awed and admiring spectators, charming young women, foreign princes, respectful easterners, was to give scope to whatever latent sense of the histrionic was in a man; it gave opportunity to satisfy a desire for fine, even gaudy, raiment since the pilot was expected to dress as befitted his high station. Most important of all perhaps, the job paid a large salary and therefore measured up to the chief standard of the time, which was money. As long as the pilot had a job, he was his own master, a law unto himself, and his pilots' association gave him considerable assurance of a steady job, or at least a steady income. On top of all this he enjoyed extensive leisure in the gay, wicked city of New Orleans, careless leisure in which to air his greatness in the billiard room and bar of the Planters' Hotel in Saint Louis.

The young pilot Sam Clemens was deliriously happy; it shows in his letters of the period. He could afford a "ten dollar dinner" at a French restaurant in New Orleans. He could take his mother and two girls, one of them his cousin, on a trip to New Orleans and show them the sights as one long familiar with the city. He could send his mother money in almost every letter that he wrote home. He could take a grim pleasure in displaying his success before those who had doubted his ability. He was so happy that he was afraid to boast of his happiness for fear it might be destroyed.

The destruction of the world of the river occurred as though by magic. It had been in preparation for many years but when it came, it came swiftly, with a finality that amazed the people who were part of this world and who had looked upon it as eternal and indivisible. On one day the boats went up the river as they always had, the world went forward. And on the next day there was simply chaos, sprawling, bloody chaos. Sam Clemens took the only wise and sensible course; he left the universe which had crumbled into ruins. Forever after he would be an alien, but he would carry with him the memory of this separate world in which he had received such rich rewards. He would look in vain for those rewards in literature, in business, in a half dozen other fields. They were the rewards of a special way of life that had gone forever.

7

Rivalry of the Railroads

The boom on the Mississippi served in its inception to intensify the sense of dominion that was the heritage of the people who lived along the river. Here was a bond of union as lasting as the earth itself, linking North and South beyond all petty dissension, beyond the momentary strife of party and faction.

There were those, of course, who wanted to believe this, who clung to the faith that the Mississippi system was vital to the economic life of both the North and the South. And since this was so, they argued, how could any minor issue such as slavery disrupt the union? Was not the section through which the Mississippi flowed the very heart of the confederation, the stream that drew its lifeblood from all the states of the union?

So went a prevailing and hopeful kind of rhetoric. "The federal constitution cannot be overthrown while the Mississippi states remain in convention and harmony," said one Daniel Drake before the Literary Convention of Kentucky in the chapel of Transylvania University in 1833. It began early and continued late, this fervent hope that the Mississippi, as though by some magic in its very waters, might arrest the maggot of disunion.

A set of practical politicians — one may well assume that they were practical — The Democratic-Republican Young Men's General Committee of Tammany Hall in New York, paid no small sum in 1850 to print five thousand copies of *The King of Rivers, with a Chart of Our Slave and Free Soil Territory*. The author of *The King of Rivers* was Cora Montgomery, who devel-

oped in lofty language the thesis that the river was an eternal
bond. The North might abuse the Indian and the South might
cry shame, as the North cried out against the enslavement of the
black man, but this would not alter the fact that "fourteen powerful states and nearly half our entire population" were coursed
by the great river. The Mississippi was a "silver zone," said Miss
Montgomery, binding "varied climes to one common interest."
"No fraction of the wide territory enfolded in the embrace of the
hundred armed river ... could cut itself from the rest of the
body, without destroying the growth and vigor of its own fair
proportions."

Southern writers were particularly fond of reciting the imper-
ishable virtues of the Mississippi. Southern journals were filled
with their eulogies. "The Nile itself," said one ardent rhetorician,
"in its greatest usefulness, never approached in importance this
river, Mississippi. Had its geographical direction been east and
west instead of what it is, it might have become a barrier between
the northern and southern states; but happily for us it is a perpetual bond of union, by its rise, its direction, and its terminus, and
we should be the most ungrateful of nations if we did not so con-
sider it."

In large part this was the insistent wish of a South that saw its
economic life, in which the river was an accident most fortuitous
and convenient, gravely menaced. The time when Northwest
and Southwest had been bound by deep ties of real self-interest
in the river was so recent that even those who were not beguiled
into wishful thinking could hardly accept the obvious facts that
pointed to the sundering of these ties. As late as 1846 there gathered at a great river convention at Memphis representatives from
every southern and western state and the Territory of Iowa,
which sent its most distinguished citizen, General Dodge. The
delegates worked in harmony of purpose, according to the official reports, that transcended all political differences. They
united "on the leading principles of a convention not second to
any which has assembled since the adoption of the Federal Constitution."

One may see here, perhaps for the last time, the dominion of

the river, made up of the states contiguous to it and its tributaries, conscious of its oneness and its integrity, aware of its
strength and its potential power. What these delegates wanted
was money from Congress for river improvement. Congress had
failed them, and again and again. Since that first appropriation
in 1824, when $105,000 had been granted to Captain Henry
Shreve to clear the snags out of the river, Congress had grown
more and more niggardly. And the reason was not far to seek.

It lay in the East. In the East were powerful men who looked
with envious eyes upon the river trade of the West and South.
These powers had been endeavoring for more than twenty years,
ever since the inception of the Erie Canal, to steal this trade.
Night and day they labored to draw it off to their own advantage.
They used their powers upon Congress to defeat appropriations
for the improvement of the river system. Such was the tone of the
oratory that poured out like the floodwaters of the Mississippi itself over the assembled delegates. It was difficult to check this
flow of oratory; there were champions of all the rivers in the system — the Red, the Illinois, the Tennessee, the Osage, the Ohio,
the Des Moines. And each champion advanced his own river.

Hardly an orator who did not rebuke the East. And the East
meant New York, Philadelphia, Boston. South Carolina's delegates said that these ports had drawn off the trade of her Charles-
ton. They had improved their harbors with government appropriations, they had used their hoarded capital to lure away the
trade of the South. The delegates from the southern seaboard
were full of plans to link the Southwest and the ports along the
southern Atlantic seaboard. A railroad that sought to connect the
southern seaboard with the Mississippi valley was most important in every particular, said Henry Clay. He could envision the
day when the Pacific coast, too, would pour its tribute of trade
into the Mississippi valley. "In the end the commerce of both
would be commanded and the great valley become the center of
the commerce of the world as well as of our great union if we
shall preserve our liberty and our free popular institutions." One
delegate introduced a resolution demanding that the seat of the

federal government be removed to the West, but the consensus of
the convention was that in this request he had gone too far.
There were like conventions all up and down the river during
the next few years. Particularly to the north they sought to im-
prove the Mississippi system, demanding their rights of Congress, pointing out their dependence upon inland rivers. Evansville, Indiana had such a convention in 1850 and sent a
formidable memorial to Washington, reciting the vast steamboat
tonnage on western waters and urging a liberal appropriation for
clearing out the snags and sawyers of the Ohio and Mississippi
rivers. Further, it was the plain duty of Congress, said the
Evansville memorial, to name a scientific commission to study
the causes of steamboat explosions. At Burlington, Iowa, in the
following year assembled delegates from Illinois, Missouri, Wisconsin, Iowa, and the Territory of Minnesota, who resolved:

> That the Mississippi River is a great National Highway,
> the control and jurisdiction of which has been reserved to
> Congress; and that it is the duty of the National Legislature
> to make such an improvement in the navigation of said river
> as will place our commerce upon an equal footing with that
> of the Atlantic States of this Union.
>
> That the interests of nine States and one territory impera-
> tively demand the prompt action of Congress, in making
> adequate appropriation for the removal of the obstruction
> of the navigation of the Mississippi River, formed by the
> Des Moines and Rock River Rapids.

But for all the oratory and the fine ardor of the gentlemen assembled in convention, the river would be severed, would be
broken. It was essentially a southern river, its greatest commerce
dependent upon the cotton-and-slavery system of the South.
There was no vital effort to weld the province of the river into an
integral economic whole — the oratory of southern gentlemen to
the contrary — so long as the cotton crop yielded its generous reward to the few who were ostensibly leaders in the South. Along
the northern reaches of the Mississippi, above Saint Louis, an-

other kind of life was coming into being; there they would not wait upon southern indifference, southern lethargy; they would not long heed the rhetoric of southern orators.

The Yankees, those powerful, pushing men from the East, offered them railroads. Chicago, young, aggressive Chicago, had begun to thrust out the first western lines; soon they would touch the banks of the great river at seven points. And behind them and linked with them was the system of eastern railroads, lakes, and canals that had been carrying to New York an ever greater share of the produce of the West, the produce that had once flowed down the river to New Orleans.

It is above all in the province of the river that one may see the conflict sharply drawn between the expanding capitalist industrialism of the North — dominated by New York, Philadelphia, Boston — and the feudal cotton-and-slavery system of the South. "I do not promise," wrote an Iowan in 1850 to one in Saint Louis who was committed to the river system, "that the sympathies of this vicinity will not be with the East, in an effort to probe the undine region and the coteau des prairies of Niccolet, before our heads are grey. Yankee enterprise is coming to teach our 'young ideas how to shoot.' " Yankee enterprise was creating even larger and larger surpluses of capital in Yankee factories and this Yankee capital was going into iron rails, binding the West to the East with a tie that was far more potent than a flowing river; the tie of ownership, of self-interest, of plunder in a province now seen to be of incalculable wealth. "To teach our 'young ideas how to shoot.' " — in that casual expression is an accidental irony that encompasses a great deal of history — the surrender of Appomattox and much of what happened after.

I have tried to show that the river system was inefficient, chaotic, so highly individualistic that no form of discipline or control was possible. It was also given to the exploitation of narrow monopolies. Wharfage charges were exorbitant and unreasonable. As early as 1835 the duties on steam and flatboats at New Orleans amounted in one year to $76,981. "The whole of your wharfage fees, port charges, etc." said a letter written to *De Bow's Review,* published in New Orleans in 1851, "are infinitely too high." The writer compared them to similar charges in New York, Boston, Philadelphia. And this was a frequent complaint. There were repeated demands that New Orleans create a system of public covered wharves. Because of the lack of such wharves, goods were often left to the mercy of the weather. Draying and warehouse companies made large profits.

In the same way, shippers and those who had the interests of the river at heart railed at the careless system of freight tariffs. By 1851 carrying charges on the river system had increased out of all proportion. At a Chicago waterways convention the previous year it had been pointed out that the cost of transporting freight by western rivers was almost five times the cost on Lake Erie.

Besides the slovenliness of the system, there were absurd and unreasonable inequalities. For example, the rate between New Orleans and Memphis was on the average 50 percent higher than the rate between New Orleans and Pittsburgh; and this in the face of the obvious fact that navigation to Memphis, a distance of eight hundred miles, was safe and easy, while the river between Memphis and Pittsburgh, twelve hundred miles, was difficult and dangerous. Critics said that the New Orleans-Memphis rate should be no more than one-fourth that of the New Orleans-Pittsburgh charge. There was no coordination, no real system of rates at all.

While many, perhaps the majority, were complacent in the face of these abuses, under the seeming impression that the river was a perpetual part of an eternal order, there were those who were deeply concerned over the fate of the section of which the river was the center. And grave cause existed for their concern. The census of 1850 showed that New Orleans had dropped from third place to seventh place, its rate of growth only about 45 percent, "far below the rate of any other city in the Union of equal magnitude." What was even more alarming was the fact — and there were those who said that statistics proved it to be a fact — that the trade of New Orleans showed an actual decline. A comparison of trade for 1849 and 1850 disclosed that 572 fewer flatboats and eighty-nine fewer steamboats had put in at the New Orleans wharf in the latter year, a decline of 65,677 tons. Others

pointed out that if over a longer period of time the trade of New
Orleans had not shown an actual decline, the increase was not in
proportion with the great expansion that had occurred in the
West. Nor was it comparable to the increase in receipts of western produce that New York had enjoyed.

There lay the rub. In 1842, there had come by the canal system
to New York western produce of the value of $22,751,013. Eight
years later this figure had jumped to $55,474,937, a gain of ap-
proximately 120 percent, a comparative increase by New York of
25 percent over New Orleans. And in this period of fabulous expansion New Orleans's comparative loss was deeply significant,
as a few discerning individuals were aware.

> It is not many years since we were laughed at for predict-
> ing the probable decline of New Orleans. The opinion had
> become almost universal, in both Europe and America, that
> New Orleans was destined to rival the greatest commercial
> cities on the globe. This opinion was plausible and it re-
> quired the strongest kind of evidence — palpable demon-
> stration — to change it; nor was the fact generally admitted,
> that the commerce of New Orleans did not keep pace with
> the increase of commodities in the interior, until it was pro-
> mulgated by her own citizens. . . . It may be questioned
> whether, in a time of peace and general prosperity, a parallel
> of commercial decline can be found in the whole history of
> commerce.

It was obvious to a few, even in the South, that each new connection, canal or railroad, between East and West would drain
off more of the trade of the Mississippi. As early as 1850 it was
noted that the merchants of Lake Providence, Vicksburg, and
Natchez on the lower river had begun to receive a portion of
their goods from the East by the northern route, through the
canals and over the railroads of Pennsylvania, Ohio, and Illinois.
In 1851 it was reported that the freight down the river from
above the falls of the Ohio would be much less than in previous
years because in the previous season shippers had discovered
they could send their produce to market in New York far more

swiftly and more cheaply than by the Mississippi to New Orleans. On the Cincinnati stock exchange the New Orleans reports were neglected for those from New York, which determined Cincinnati prices. The new railway from Cincinnati to Sandusky on Lake Erie was able to carry only a fraction of the freight offered to it; a special force of three hundred men worked on additional cars.

The Wabash and Erie Canal was stretching its line down the banks of the Wabash and sweeping the whole products of the valley up the river against its natural current, to the eastern markets by way of the Lakes. The Illinois Canal had carried off the grain grown in the valley of the Illinois River, which had always, until the construction of the canal, passed down the Mississippi. In 1851 it was predicted that the pork and beef of the region would take the same route this spring. A short time before, the Galena and Chicago Railway had opened and it was gathering the lead of Galena and Dubuque and the produce of northern Illinois, directing it to the East, instead of floating it to the South on the broad current of the Mississippi as before. As if all this was not enough, another railroad had been surveyed to pass through central Illinois and Indiana, from Saint Louis to Cincinnati. Railways were projected by Maryland, Virginia, and South Carolina to reach into all the river valleys. And these were the projects of eastern capital, never mistaken in its aim.

There were varied reactions to this radical shift that was occurring with such astonishing rapidity. Some saw in it a kind of villainy on the part of the East; as though it had been part of a conscious, carefully prepared plot to gain tyrannical ascendancy. In the South and the Southwest particularly, the trend of travel and trade from east to west, as opposed to north and south, was regarded as an abhorrent process, in defiance of the decrees of nature. Over and over it was emphasized that the Mississippi was the "natural channel"; that in the movement from north to south there was exchanged the products of different climates, that the very existence of rivers must inevitably determine the direction of exchange.

But even at New Orleans there was some understanding of the

plain fact that a human equation was also involved. The men of the South, whether from the influence of their environment or from some inherent difference in the stock that settled the region, hardly concerned themselves with trade. It was recognized that a kind of absenteeism had grown up in New Orleans. Representatives of eastern firms carried on a great deal of the business of the town, remitting their profits to banks in New York. And for all that certain Jeremiahs preached the dangers of this absenteeism, it was difficult to make New Orleans understand what it meant: that the trade that flowed through the city in no way contributed to its upbuilding, scarcely to its sustenance. Others throughout the South urged the establishment of manufacturers, pointing to the need for industries if communities were to be built up. But few heard and fewer heeded. Cotton each year rolled up its white tide of wealth, the planters bought Sèvres vases for their mantels, sent their sons abroad for foreign culture, followed the season from White Sulphur to Saratoga with an interlude in New Orleans. They were content with life.

Railroads had become the approved way to prosperity and all through the West schemes and projects were begun, most of them colored with that high American hope which has so often glimmered on the distant horizon. As there had been river conventions, so now there were railroad conventions that considered the growing dominance of the East. There were ardent promoters who spoke of the Mississippi as "that mainstem" of a railroad system that should have its center in New Orleans. Those most concerned over southern losses sought to encourage New Orleans capital in the development of railroad lines that should feed river ports such as Memphis. Thus, it was argued, there would be preserved at least a part of the trade that was threatened from the East.

With this went a frank acknowledgment that the Northwest was lost. No matter; the river above Memphis is frozen one half the year and dry the other half went the argument of those who believed the South must take swift and drastic means to hold what trade remained. Conventions, railroad and river, no longer included both southern and western states. The South abandoned Iowa, Illinois, Wisconsin, Minnesota, and concentrated on measures to preserve the lower Mississippi from the invader. Even northern Missouri, it was said, was threatened by the East. "And you might as well try to confine a powdermill after the match has been applied, as attempt to coop up Yankee skill and enterprise. This trade, if not secured, will depart and much of it pass by way of the Lakes to New York." Others held that the whole valley might still be consolidated, the province of the river welded together again, if only it were possible to build, without appeal to eastern capitalists, a railroad from Saint Paul to New Orleans. The new, efficient, swift form of transportation would bring about what the river in its time had accomplished. This and other ambitious schemes were brought forward as the East continued to raid territory after territory, the whole movement of travel and trade shifting as though a great magnet had exerted an irresistible force upon the entire field of American life. Some said that the federal government should be compelled to deepen the mouth of the Mississippi so that larger oceangoing vessels might be persuaded to call at New Orleans instead of at New York. Then, so this plan went, the river towns as far as Alton could become ports of call, receiving foreign goods in their own customs-houses, collecting duty and carrying on their finances independent of New York and Philadelphia.

While a great many cried out against the trespasses of the East, only a few sharper, keener minds seem to have understood the real significance of what was occurring. It was the rare person who was sufficiently detached from the obscurantism of the South and the heedless, aggressive expansion of the West to appreciate what was by the middle fifties an all but accomplished fact. One man's prophetic insight into the meaning of these changes should have won him more than the oblivion that followed upon the end of his modest career.

Micajah Tarver began his *Western Journal and Civilian* in Saint Louis in 1845 and continued it until the sheriff overtook him for debt nearly ten years later. Throughout that decade, in almost every issue of his monthly journal, he shows an extraordinary awareness of the profound changes that were occurring in

America. He understood quite clearly that no political compromise could ever hold the North and the South together. He understood the invasion from the East with all its implications. He saw that western railroads built with eastern capital served only to make the West an economic fiefdom of the East. And since he had known and loved the West, the West that had been composed however momentarily of North and South, joined by the river, he tried to show what this economic dependence would mean. He foresaw all the implications of economic provincialism and absenteesim, the fatal concentration of wealth in one center that would constantly drain off the life — in money, intelligence, skill, talent — of the rest of the country.

It was not that Micajah Tarver would have hitched the West to the feudal cotton-and-slavery system of the South. In his editorials he pointed out again and again the plain fact that though the West gained population by hundreds and thousands each month, each week, each day, there had been no proportionate gain in political power; if anything, the West had lost prestige, becoming more and more a pawn in the intense struggle between the North and South, between the expanding industrialism of the one and the stubborn feudalism of the other. What was to happen in America has rarely been related more effectively.

"Eternal vigilance is the price of liberty!" he wrote.

> The cost of transportation and other charges incident to the exchange of commodities at so great a distance (that is, manufactured goods and raw materials between the Eastern seaboard and the West), is only one amongst the many evils of such a trade: the finances and circulation of money, throughout the entire system, are controlled by the operation at the chief commercial point, whither money is attracted by laws not less certain than those of gravitation. Owing to the influence of these laws, capital never accumulates in districts remote from the great commercial centre, to an extent sufficient to attract the arts and embellish either the country or its towns; and hence, all, who possess time

and means for the enjoyment of fashionable luxuries, flock to the great commercial emporium; and expend there, or within its immediate vicinity, the small profits which have been saved, with much care, from their pursuits in the interior. And in time this custom becomes so firmly established that one who has never spent a season at the metropolis is in danger of losing caste in that society esteemed most respectable in the country; and therefore many whose means do not justify the expense of a pilgrimage to the east are compelled to go thither for the purpose of sustaining their social position. Thus, in many respects, under the present system, which is daily gaining strength, the Western States are subjected to the relation of Provinces of the east; they are drained of the capital created here as fast as it accumulates; the productive properties of their soil are exhausted to furnish bread and other commodities to the manufacturers and artizans of that region; the attachment of the people for their homes and their immediate social relations are weakened by a comparison of the rude conditions of things around them with the luxuries and artificial refinements of eastern cities; and withal our public policy receives its direction and is, in a great measure, controlled by those residing east of the Alleghenies. And so it must be ever under the present system. For there is an affinity, and we might say almost an identity, between political and commercial power, by virtue whereof the former is modified and controlled more than by written constitutions or legislative enactments.

It is important that one person should have stated with such force and clarity precisely what was occurring, that the relation between economics and geography — a relation too little understood — should have been so concisely pointed out in the year 1854. Behind the loud reverberations of the slavery issue, the West — Wisconsin, Illinois, Iowa, Minnesota, the states along the upper Mississippi — was being bound tighter and tighter to the industrial capitalism that was owned and controlled in the

East. Against this attack the river system, scarcely a system at all, was powerless. The set of habits, traditions, and loyalties that had grown up around a means of transportation established by an accident of geography retained for a time a certain coherence, a certain identity. But the vitality, the reason for the existence of the river system had been destroyed. The dominion of the river was shattered before it had come into being.

8

The Bridge

While the steamboats continued, with the swelling tide of cotton and the boom in Minnesota, to do a thriving business, it is perhaps no exaggeration to say that by the middle fifties they had begun to take on an air of the curious and the antiquarian. The railroad was the new, swift, efficient, fashionable mode of travel. *Lloyd's Steamboat Directory* for 1856 gives more space to railroads than to steamboats. Passengers for the West might make connections with a great number of western railroads for a variety of points, and "also with the Steam Packet boats to and from New Orleans, St. Louis, Louisville, and Cincinnati."

There was a Railway Line of packets, controlled by railway capital, which advertised a degree of efficiency and speed rivaling that of the cars. The schedule of the Railway Line was arranged to coincide with the arrival of passenger trains from the East. Futile demands were made in Saint Louis and New Orleans for a coordinated line of freight boats that would recapture with lowered rates a part of the heavy carrying trade that had been lost. Hope was dwindling among those who had been most ardent in behalf of the river system. Angry political tempers served in part to obscure economic losses.

But in the spring of 1856 an event occurred which river men could not ignore. A bridge was completed across the Mississippi River from the town of Rock Island, Illinois to Davenport, Iowa. The same interests that had furthered the Erie Canal, that had developed the trade of the Lakes, that had pushed railroads

across western prairies and into western river valleys now
spanned the great Mississippi, the great river. In some quarters
there was cause for rejoicing, Chicago boasted in the arrogant
way in which Chicago always boasted. "The Mississippi River
Crossed By The Iron Horse," said the headline in the *Chicago
Democratic Press.* "Great Rejoicing . . . The Greatest Feat of the
Nineteenth Century." From the beginning of time, said Chicago,
the mighty Mississippi has rolled on, unchallenged, and now we
have put a bridge across its waters, stemmed its current with the
piers of that bridge. Chicago knew from the first that its destiny
was hitched to the progress of the railroads.

Those who crossed on the first train felt the import of the hour.
"Passengers for Iowa keep their seats," an official called out.
There was a silence described as "solemn." And then when the
last car was safe on the Iowa shore, a mighty shout went up,
"We're over, we're over!" And Chicago said, "Yes, the Missis-
sippi is practically no more."

But the Mississippi and the thousands of men who made their
living on the river were not to surrender without a struggle. The
contest over the first bridge, the early skirmishes bitterly fought
out long before the span itself was completed, embodies the
whole opposition between the river system and the railroad system, between the individualistic, chaotic South and West and the
corporate, efficient East. It was a contest predestined by all the
force of circumstance, as inevitable as the war between the states
that followed so soon after. It was a futile struggle fought long
after the essential issue of victory was resolved. And yet it is revealing of the solid economic shapes that projected such large
political shadows, and was, in its very futility, dramatic and
moving.

In the early fifties the firm of Sheffield and Farnam had completed construction of the Michigan Southern Railroad to Chicago, and this was but a preface to the building of the Chicago,
Rock Island and Pacific Railroad to the Mississippi River. Sheffield retired to become patron of the scientific school at Yale that
bears his name. Henry Farnam, with the aid of the eastern capitalists who had sponsored his earlier projects and with the lesser

support of a group of men in Iowa and Illinois, projected a rail-road that should cross the Mississippi, traverse Iowa, and reach the banks of the Missouri at Council Bluffs. It was a bold plan, typical of the projects that Farnam and the capitalists associated with him had pushed to completion. They were vigorous, ruthless men who let nothing stand in the way of their ambition. The country was enjoying an amazing prosperity and the surplus was theirs to invest in western expansion.

It was not difficult in this instance to get what they needed. The Illinois legislature authorized construction of the first span, which would extend from the town Rock Island, on the Illinois shore, to Rock Island, the government-owned seat of a fort and arsenal. Permission to build the longest span, from the island to the Iowa shore was readily granted by the Iowa legislature. The channel of the river, which was here very swift and turbulent, ran along the western side of the island. Six massive stone piers, three within the Iowa boundary and three on the Illinois bottom, were to be built to support a wooden superstructure. Approximately in the middle there would be a great pier — with a width of 45 feet and a length, including the guard piers, of 386 feet — to carry the revolving section of the bridge. This turntable was necessary, of course, to permit the steamboats, with their tall scrollwork smokestacks, to pass through. Lumber rafts and boats without stacks could go through the ordinary spans.

The very proposal of such a bridge aroused an immediate fury of protest. There were many who said that it was impossible, that the fierce current of the Mississippi would dash down whatever man might set in its way. Others, with a knowledge of the miracles performed by the railroad builders, began to organize an opposition. This opposition brought such pressure to bear in Washington that the secretary of war ordered the U.S. district attorney for northern Illinois to apply for an injunction to prevent the construction of the railroad across Rock Island near the government's fort. The question of the obstruction that the bridge would offer to navigation was also raised. After lengthy argument, the presiding judge, John McLean, an associate justice of the Supreme Court, denied the injunction the government had asked. The case of *United States* v. *Railroad Bridge Company* was so decided in July of 1855 and from that date construction was pushed at top speed.

The opposition prior to completion of the bridge in April of the following year was nothing compared to the outcry that arose from the whole fraternity of steamboatmen when the piers were in place and the long span completed. Owners, captains, and pilots claimed that it virtually put an end to navigation of the upper river. It was their charge that the railroad company had deliberately set out to destroy the navigability of the Mississippi by placing the great pier in such a way that treacherous currents eddied and swirled around it. The two piers that spanned the channel were the Scylla and Charybdis of the river and, so rivermen said, many a brave boat and many a brave man would go down near their perilous waters.

On the night of May 4, the steamboat *Effie Afton,* captain, J. S. Hurd, reached Rock Island bound upriver for Saint Paul. She was a brand new boat with a large cargo of freight and passengers. Several other boats, among them the *Tishomingo,* the *Kate Paulding,* the *Hamburg,* the *Clara Dean,* the *Mattie Wayne,* the *Ben Bolt* and the *J. B. Carson,* lay at Rock Island waiting, as the *Effie Afton* was forced to, for the wind to die. It had been blowing hard from the northeast, which made it impossible to run the bridge. Two boats, impatient with waiting, attempted the following day to make the passage in the face of the wind and failed.

Early in the morning of the second day, the wind having subsided, the *J. B. Carson* started for the span. But the *Effie Afton,* according to one passenger, "walked past us like a thing of life and got into the gap ahead of us." She got about halfway through when the watch on the *Carson* saw that her stern was caught in one of the whirlpools that eddied around the long pier. The pilot on duty made a valiant effort to hold her to a straight course but the boat was like a chip in the violent current sweeping under the bridge. Onlookers on the *Carson* saw the helpless boat driven first against one pier, then the other. For an instant they thought she might save herself, but the rushing water drove her a third time onto the pier on her starboard side. A fearful crash followed and almost immediately, the screams of passengers thrown out of their berths.

The final crash had lodged the *Effie Afton* against the starboard pier. She careened at an angle of forty-five degrees and it seemed that, with the water swirling over her hold, she must go over at any moment. Captain Brickle of the *Carson* put the bow of his boat against the afterguards of the *Afton* and began to assist in the rescue of passengers and crew. Fortunately the *Afton* had lodged in such a way that many could escape by climbing up onto the bridge; deck passengers scrambled onto the *Carson.* In a remarkably short time the *Afton* was cleared of her passengers and most of her crew. There were reports after the disaster that at least five men had drowned, but these were never verified.

And then it was seen that the fire that had broken out when the stoves had upset in the first crash could not be checked. The flames mounted high, the poor animals confined on the lower deck began to scream. In a few minutes the wooden span of the bridge had caught fire. The half-naked passengers who had fled to that refuge ran wildly for safety. The *Carson* was endangered but finally cut herself free as someone raised the cry that there was powder in the *Afton*'s hold. Bridge and boat burned fiercely with the awful sound of the trapped cattle and horses rising above the crackling and hissing of the fire itself.

The fire had blazed scarcely ten minutes when the wooden span, one mass of flames, crashed down onto the burning boat. This released the ruined *Afton,* which was whirled crazily downstream, a floating pyre. With the crash of the bridge the whistles on every boat in sight were opened wide in one long, sustained peal of triumph. On the shore women rang dinner bells, men shouted in a frenzy of excitement.

There was nothing to stop any steamboat now. On her way upstream the *Hamburg* made and flew a flag that had painted on it the legend: "Mississippi Bridge Destroyed. Let All Rejoice." River men actually believed in the exultation of the moment that this might be the end of the whole project. "It is to be hoped," said the *Galena Advertiser,* that the Directors of the Company will now allow their better judgment to prevail and remove the remaining obstructions. The fact that, during the short time since navigation commenced this spring, the losses sustained by shipping in consequence of the obstruction cannot fall much short of one hundred thousand dollars, must be taken as positive proof that the structure is where it should not be, and where it cannot, in justice, any longer remain than the time required by the owners to remove it. It has been built in the wrong place.

River men little understood the railroad builders.

Within less than four months the span from Rock Island to the Iowa shore had been replaced. All up and down the river they prepared for the next trial of strength in this warfare between steamboat and railroad. Captain Hurd, who had put his life savings into the *Effie Afton,* sued the railroad company for the loss of his boat. And the men of his calling came to his aid, realizing full well that the case was a critical one for all who made a living in the river trade. Distinguished counsel was marshaled on both sides. The railroad company had as one of their lawyers Abraham Lincoln of Springfield, who had won a great many railway cases in Illinois. Another Lincoln, T. D. of Cincinnati, a more distinguished attorney than the Springfield circuit rider, was among Captain Hurd's counsel.

The case came to trial in United States District Court in Chicago in September of 1857, with Justice McLean again presiding. It was a trial that not only the valley but the whole nation watched. Newspapers in Saint Louis and New Orleans sent special correspondents to cover it. Very early, with the selection of a jury, it was plain that intense sectional interests were involved. Many jurors frankly admitted to sectional prejudice; several said that their businesses would be hurt if the bridge were declared a nuisance. The delegations from Saint Louis and the other river towns heard this with anxiety. Chicago hardly seemed the place for such a trial.

The opening statement for Captain Hurd was made by H. M.

Weed of Peoria. They would show, he said, that the railroad had deliberately placed the great pier in such a way as to create an obstruction to navigation. It was not that they opposed all bridges, this was not a war on bridges. "We do not say," he added, "that a bridge may not be built at Rock Island which will accommodate the wants of the railroad and the wants of river navigation also." N. B. Judd, in his opening statement for the defense, claimed that they could prove that the *Effie Afton* was racing for the draw with the *J. B. Carson.* "And as they were insured only against fire she was set fire to."

"We say," Mr. Judd thundered out in the crowded courtroom, "that the pilots have combined as one man almost, and we are here today resting upon the science which does not lie. Why should we have to appear here to defend this case with the entire river interests from Pittsburgh to Saint Paul, under the lead of the Saint Louis Chamber of Commerce, organized at a meeting held on the sixteenth of December?"

"You really do not state that?" Mr. Lincoln of Cincinnati interrupted.

"I state it is in your depositions," Mr. Judd said in answer, "that Captain Hudson, who was the leading spirit said that this suit must be vigorously pursued, because a decision in this case might prevent their tearing down all the other bridges. I have read it. I say, then, with the influence of the Chamber of Commerce, beginning with last December, pressing out of employment any pilot that dares to express his true opinion, that thing has been organized from Pittsburgh to Saint Louis, and — well, I've seen them myself as I stood upon the bridge.

"A boat came up there and for the purpose of creating public opinion that they cannot get through, the captain sends the passengers all off around the bridge because it is dangerous. But as soon as their passengers are off, they lower their buckets and come kiting up through the bridge. Why do they do this? So that passengers may go and tell half the world what a great danger they have been in from this bridge."

It was useless to deny these charges. The meeting at Saint Louis had even been reported in the papers, although there had been some attempt to keep it secret at least in part. At that time such ardent defenders of the river system as Thomas B. Hudson had sought to rally a united front against the encroachments of the railroads. There had been speeches, violent in their denunciation of the railroads and the eastern capitalists who foisted them upon the West. If the Rock Island bridge was allowed to stand, "then no power on earth can prevent the people of Hannibal, Quincy, and above Davenport and Dubuque, from being bridged over by these obstructions to the free commerce of the world." It was pointed out that the insurance companies at Cincinnati had added one percent to their rates for those boats that must run through the bridge. This amounted to as much as $1,300 a day, which, it was said, the railroad company should be made to pay.

Technical witnesses for both sides passed in a procession across the witness stand. The defense experts sought to show, through a series of tests they had made with floats, that it was no more difficult to run through the bridge than it was to run any other stretch of swift water. And the experts employed by Captain Hurd had equally good evidence to show that the piers of the bridge created a small maelstrom that was ready to suck down even the wariest and most skillful of pilots. That has apparently been the way of expert witnesses since the beginning of time. There were acrimonious exchanges when feelings flared beyond the techncial confines of the law.

The sober words of Abraham Lincoln were in behalf of reason, moderation, compromise. He had no prejudice, he said, against steamboats or steamboatmen, nor any against Saint Louis, for he supposed they went about as other people would do in their situation. So far as he could see, the meetings in Saint Louis were connected with the case only because some witnesses had attended them, and thus had some prejudice and color to their testimony. The last thing that would be pleasing to him would be to have one of those great channels, extending almost from where it never freezes to where it never thaws, blocked up. But, he was quick to add, there is a travel from east to west whose demands are not less important than those of the river. It is growing larger and larger, said the prairie lawyer, building up new states with a rapidity never before seen in the history of the world.

He supported this with facts and figures. Illinois had grown within his memory to a population of a million and a half. Iowa and the other young communities of the Northwest were developing with extraordinary swiftness. This current of travel, he said again, has its rights as well as that of north and south. If the river had the advantage in priority and legislation, we could nevertheless enter into free competition with it and we would surpass it. Why, he said, it was in the evidence that from September 8, 1856 to August 8, 1857, 12,586 freight cars and 74,179 passengers had passed over this bridge. What was more, the river was blocked by ice at least four months of the year. And when they talked of building a tunnel under the river or a suspension bridge high above it, they were talking of what was highly impractical and costly. So he concluded and eased his lanky figure into a chair.

This calm council fell upon deaf ears. The prejudices and hopes and fears of the South were too close to the river and the destiny of the river to accept a compromise. There was apprehension over Justice McLean's charge to the jury, a murmuring from the river delegations. "Bountiful as providence has been in supplying our country with great lakes and mighty rivers, they are found inadequate to the wants of society. . . . New fields of industry and enterprise necessarily open up new avenues of intercourse. This is the law of progress. . . . And however sectional jealousy may arise out of this progress, it will be seen and acknowledged that the prosperity of the whole country is consistent with the prosperity of its different parts." And when the jury returned a verdict in favor of the railroads there was an angry clamor in the courtroom. Chicago had defeated justice, said the river men, but they would find another court.

In May of the following year James M. Ward, a Saint Louis steamboatman, filed a bill in the federal court for the southern division of Iowa asking that the bridge be declared a nuisance and ordered removed. Again there was voluminous testimony, and this time the men of the river got a favorable decision. Judge

John M. Love declared that the bridge was in fact "a common and public nuisance," holding further that there was involved "a question of public policy as well as private right." This decision was handed down in November of 1859. Judge Love commented on the fact that bridges were contemplated at Dubuque and Lyons and that probably McGregor, La Crosse, Muscatine, Burlington, Keokuk, Quincy, Hannibal, and Saint Louis would follow. "Thus," he said, "if this precedent be established, we shall probably, in no great period of time, have railroad bridges upon the Mississippi River at every forty or fifty miles of its course."

Once more there was celebration along the river, and again the celebration was premature. Counsel for the railroad well knew that this was not the end. Judge Love had ordered the three piers on the Iowa side removed, but not one stone was disturbed. Instead there was begun the lengthy process of appeal, which automatically stayed the order of the lower court. The final decision, for the railroads it is hardly necessary to add, was to come three years later — a superfluous blessing for an event that had long since transpired. A nation torn by rebellion must have wondered what ancient cause this was that the old men of the Supreme Court had finally gotten around to deciding.

Meanwhile, on almost any stretch of the river between Saint Paul and New Orleans you could see the black plume of smoke that meant flourishing steamboat trade, a prosperity that continued, thanks to cotton, even after the collapse in 1857. The men of the river were touched by the slavery issue only indirectly. They were for settlement, for compromise; they could not believe in rebellion. Life went on. Pilots displayed themselves, their airs and graces, their finery, in the billiard room of the Planters', at Antoine's and La Louisianne. A gentleman of Natchez was building what was to be the finest residence in the South — octagonal if you please, six stories high, with thirty-two octagonal rooms and niches all about for marble statues that had been ordered from Italy.

Then one day an amazing thing happened. The *Uncle Sam* was bound up the river from New Orleans. There was war talk but the *Uncle Sam* was not molested. At a point below Saint

Louis, just abreast of Jefferson Barracks, she received a hail; confused voices came out over the water. The *Uncle Sam* continued on her course. Again came the shouts, as though peremptory, as though in command. With sublime indifference the *Uncle Sam* continued up the river. The next thing that happened was that a shell exploded perilously close to the pilothouse, shattering glass and gingerbread ornament.

"What in hell was that for?" said the captain.

"Damned if I know," said the pilot.

It was war — amazing, incredible war. Yankee enterprise had "taught the young idea how to shoot." The Mississippi River was practically no more.

9

The South Despairs

On the day that war was declared the river passed under the rule
of the military. All commerce, all traffic, all life gave way to the
demands of war. Factories in the industrial North whirred and
hummed at an even faster pace. Profits doubled and trebled
under the impetus of war, swelling and multiplying in the coffers
of eastern bankers. While railroad construction was curtailed, it
did not altogether cease. Men toiled and tilled and schemed and
planned, scarcely knowing even the remote breath of war. But
the river was stripped bare; only the weird, impromptu battle
fleets were left, and the commandeered boats carrying troops and
guns and supplies.

The Mississippi was at the heart of the rebellion, the scene of
important battles by land and water. From the perspective of the
present, the naval engagements on the Mississippi have a curious, half-mad, half-pathetic quality — brother fighting brother
in tubs armored with tin, pilothouses that were called slaughter
pens because there was no escape from death, great engagements
in swampy bayous and narrow reaches where men fought within
the sound of each others' voices, cracker-box flotillas that burned
like rushlights, sealing the crew and officers within small floating
hells.

For the four terrible, interminable years of the rebellion the
river was shut off; the economic system of which it was a part was
nearly dead. That trade on the river revived at all when the war

ended was proof of the integral part it had played in the life of the region.

Boat building had not ceased. Under the direction of that brilliant young engineer James B. Eads, a great many armed gunboats had slipped from the ways of a half dozen yards at Saint Louis. A number of big boats had been built at fabulous prices, and others enlarged to transport troops and munitions. But the destruction of steamboats in the South made the demand for new vessels acute; in the first six months of peace there was a great boom in the Saint Louis boatyards. Nearly forty boats were built and sent down the river for the southern trade. Levees, even ruined levees at southern ports, were for the moment crowded. It seemed as though flush times on the Mississippi had been miraculously restored.

This was only a brief, illusory reminder of the old life, stimulated by the rush of carpetbaggers into the South and the flow of settlers who had waited for the war to end. Steamboatmen up and down the river were very soon made to realize that there were too many boats in the Mississippi trade. Their trials of old with the railroads — which were now certain to offer keener and more far-flung competition — made then acutely aware that the old way of individual operation would not suffice. They must combine, they must cooperate, and in earnest now, for the haunting fear of extinction, though never expressed, was somehow always in the air.

Hardly half the tonnage on the Mississippi and the Ohio could be profitably employed. This was the dismal fact that the steamboat owners had to face as they set about to bring some kind of order out of the utter demoralization that prevailed. Numerous plans were considered and rejected by the more important owners and finally a joint stock company was agreed upon, the capital to be fixed at the assessed value of all the boats which would be included in the organization.

They made a brave beginning, as brave as their name, The Atlantic and Mississippi Steamship Company. There were twenty boats in the line, the largest and the finest then afloat;

their valuation was two and a half million, a fabulous valuation it was thought. The line had the most extensive agencies and connections of any steamboat company in the world. It had its own system of coupon tickets, good on any railroad in the country. Connections at New Orleans with New York by steamship were very close.

The officers of the boats were carried away with the grandeur and importance of their company. Subject only to slight supervision, each captain seemed to feel that it was his principal duty to excel every other boat of the line in speed, generosity of cuisine, and lavishness of decor. Greenbacks were as cheap as cabbage leaves. Terrapin appeared on menus absurdly long. Ships' officers drank still catawba wine with distinguished passengers, at company expense of course. Several went so far as to introduce — and this was considered a little effete — the new mosquito bar at the windows of their deluxe staterooms. The shower of greenbacks came down out of heaven itself and the directors of the Atlantic and Mississippi Steamship Company bought four more boats, increasing the capital stock to $2,240,000.

The *Olive Branch* was a beautiful packet, one of the finest ever built, and so was the *Ruth.* The captain of the latter gave it out to the press that he had made $42,000 in one trip from Louisville to New Orleans. But this was strong even for the heyday of greenbacks, and other captains laughed. The *Ruth* had a freight capacity of 2,500 tons, and the furniture of her public saloons was upholstered in the finest brocades. The *Ida Handy,* the *Mollie Able,* and the *Pauline Carroll* were nearly as fine. When three or four of these boats — all white and gilt, very new and gay, their black smoke plumes floating high — lay at the levee, it seemed that the river flourished as of old.

But in the very nature of this combine there were fatal flaws. It was the organization of men who had never learned how to organize. The elephant was trying to learn to dance, the lion to sing in chorus, and the process was difficult. In number, the boats excluded from the Atlantic and Mississippi Company nearly equaled those under its flag, and while they were inferior in speed and appointments they offered formidable competition, free from any of the restraints entailed in organization. And through a serious error in judgment on the part of the directors of the Atlantic and Mississippi Company this competition was focused and sharpened.

Although the war was over and the various armies had been returned to their homes, the government still had a great deal of water transportation to be done throughout the entire Mississippi valley. Bids were called for to include all this transportation over a long period of months. For some strange reason, either because they decided they had had enough of government contracts before the surrender or because they considered this business beaneath them, the directors of the Atlantic and Mississippi Steamship Company declined to put in a bid. This fat contract gave a great impetus to a second combine, which was formed with a more practical direction.

Control over individual boats and their captain-owners in the Atlantic and Mississippi line was so loose that it was almost impossible to check the extravagances that went on. Soon the public began to suspect what was actually true — that while there was a great volume of business and every outward sign of flourishing prosperity, there were no profits.

But even so, a firmer hand might have been found to enforce common sense had it not been for the overwhelming disasters that fell one after the other upon the region of the river. Plague, fire, flood, sudden death in all its manifestations came in a despairing sequence, like a second blight upon a stricken land. As an ominous portent, there had occurred, even while the ashes of the bivouac fires were yet unscattered, the fearful catastrophe of the *Sultana*. It is possible — an accurate list of the dead was never compiled — that not even the sinking of the *Titanic* took such a toll of human life, and in human suffering one may find no recorded parallel to this ghastly blunder, this incredible stupidity.

Out of Andersonville Prison in the spring of 1865 marched gray shadows, ghosts that had once been men. These prisoners, who had been held by the South since the war, were marching at long, long last to freedom, to wives, to children, to the familiar and the beloved. But marching is hardly the word; they came in a wavering, uncertain line. In cattle cars they traveled across Alabama, stopping only to put off the bodies of those who died. At Meridian in Mississippi they were told there were no more railroad facilities and they began the last stage of the journey on foot. Their goal was Vicksburg and they reached it after days of such slow, dragging torture as few men have ever endured.

At the levee lay the *Sultana*. She was a big powerful boat in the cotton trade. Beside her was the *Pauline Carroll*. The officers in charge of the troops from Andersonville marched all 1,866 men on board the *Sultana*. (Afterward, the officers were to say that the *Pauline Carroll* had employed bribery to try to get a share of the contract with the government to carry these men.) Already on board the *Sultana* were seventy cabin passengers, many of them women, eighty-five crew members, and a cargo that included numerous mules, horses, and hogs.

This was the way to freedom, to all that the men out of Andersonville had despaired of in the black, lost months. Even if they could not lie down for sheer want of enough space on the decks, even if the food was so vile and raw they could not eat it, these skeletons of men could stand in the sun, aware of their destination, aware that with each beat of the *Sultana*'s engines they were nearer to their homes. At Memphis about a hundred and fifty men, under the impression that the *Sultana* would lay over for some time, strolled up into the town. They were left behind when the boat pulled away from the levee.

Eight miles above Memphis one of the *Sultana*'s boilers exploded and flames seemed to burst out everywhere. The river was in flood, bank-full, a raging torrent of water, brown with mud and cold as ice. For half an hour a large corner of inferno was adrift, the flames crimsoning the sky, the screams of the trapped and dying shattering the night for miles around. Many of the soldiers were unable to swim at all. Those who had not been blown up or burned — there must have been eight hundred of them — gathered on the bow. The deck was pitched at a sharp angle, but the wind fanned the flames in the opposite direction. Momentarily the survivors on the bow, most of whom had stripped off their clothes and huddled stark naked, held a little hope. Then the boat swung around and the wind drove the great soaring sheet of flame down upon the naked men, searing their bodies and sending them lunging overboard in a mass. With this, the bow careened upward, and those who had not scrambled off the side in the first frenzy were hurled down into the fiery heart of the flames.

The government listed 1,258 casualties, of whom 1,101 were soldiers and the rest passengers and crew. But others said the list was nearer 1,500 dead and some put it as high as 1,900. Such horror lingers in men's minds. At the outset of the revival of the river the calamity of the *Sultana* had a profound effect, reverberating for months through official investigations and angry denunciation.

Although none of the disasters to the boats of the Atlantic and Mississippi line were of this major order, they came with appalling frequency. In fifteen months the company lost eleven splendid packets to fire, explosion, snags, collision. The steamer *W. R. Carter* blew up like a rocket twenty miles above Vicksburg in February of 1866. The blazing ruin swung around to the Arkansas shore and sank in seventy feet of water, bearing with it the charred bodies of those passengers and crew who had not been hurled into the air by the explosion, and carrying down, too, a treasure of $230,000 in a safe of the Adams Express Company. No one ever knew how many lives were lost, but only a negligible number, perhaps a half dozen, of the sixty deck passengers escaped. It was reported that all, or nearly all, of the hands of the boat, about sixty in number, had been lost.

And only a few days before, the boilers of the *Missouri,* a sister ship to the *Sultana,* had let go. The *Silver Moon* and the *Dictator* had been near enough to rescue the surviving passengers so that the toll was not quite so great. Captain Hurd of the *Missouri* had had his whole family on board, one son who was second clerk, one son who was pilot, a small boy of six, and his wife. Only Captain Hurd himself survived, and he was so flayed and tortured by the live steam that he might better have died. A current newspaper reported: "The body of Mrs. Hurd was fished up from the wreck, and was the only one that had been recovered when the *Tacony* left the place where the *Missouri* sank. Mrs. Hurd had been killed by an iron bolt which struck her on the head, smashing in her skull. The first engineer, Phillips, was blown all to pieces. All the engineers and the firemen were killed. The body of the head steward was found blown into three pieces. The first clerk, Mr. McMahon, and wife are among the killed."

So the blows fell. The *Leviathan,* the *Luna* and the *Peytona* of the Atlantic and Mississippi line lay at the Saint Louis levee. The watchman on the *Peytona* saw smoke coming from the pantry. But fire had started and the blaze spread before sleepy guards could cast out into the stream. The glow filled the whole sky and a great crown packed the levee to watch in awe this latest disaster. The *Continental,* a crack boat of the Atlantic and Mississippi combine, only narrowly escaped the conflagration. It was an ironic circumstance, not lost on the crowd watching the flames rise and fall, that the *Luna* had come into port at nine o'clock, only an hour before the fire was discovered, finding an easy berth between her sister ships, the *Leviathan* and the *Peytona.* The loss to the line was put at nearly five hundred thousand dollars.

There was no respite. The *John J. Roe* ran on a sunken wreck and was lost. The *Empress* was snagged, the *James J. White* was snagged. The *Niagara* was lost in a collision with the steamer *Post Boy.* And it had been the disastrous policy of the Atlantic and Mississippi Company to insure vessels and cargo for only a portion of their value. Damage suits multiplied so fast that counsel for the line could not keep count of them.

The belief grew along the river that the new type of tubular boiler was responsible for the fearful explosions that had occurred. The *Sultana* and the *Missouri* both had had tubular boilers. Engineers claimed that they were not as well adapted to the muddy water of the Mississippi as the old flue type. Whether there was any basis for this or whether it was merely a superstition, the prejudice of the traveling public took immediate root and the Atlantic and Mississippi line complied in laying up their finest boats to restore the older style of boiler in all. They would not "run again until all cause for uneasiness or danger, real or imaginary," had been removed. While the average American of the time seems to have been blind to it, the danger of steamboat travel was, obviously, real enough.

A haunting sense of frustration and failure hung over the river; it was in part a reflection of the misery of the South. Steamboating was not what it used to be, river men admitted when they foregathered. Memphis was plague-ridden, the stench of death in the air, thick and gray as a fog. The dying lay alone and the dead were unburied in the streets. Yellow fever was all up and down the Mississippi. The *Robert E. Lee* lay at Cairo weeks on end, waiting for the disease to abate a little so that she might be reentered in the New Orleans-Vicksburg trade. Steamboat owners, poor as they were, gave without stint to aid the stricken cities.

They kept on as long as there was even a hatful of freight, a half dozen passengers, but they could not burn hope in their furnaces nor pay their crews in future expectations. They went from day to day, always believing that at least some measure of the old abundant prosperity would return. Captain Washington of the *Ruth* wired from Louisville to the president of the Atlantic and Mississippi line: "*Ruth* here with light trip. Sixteen car-loads of hay and 200 barrels of whiskey is all the freight now in sight for shipment. Nothing coming in. Will take two weeks to load at this rate. Shall I lay her up or commence loading? Rates ruinous. I can promise nothing. Can unload tonight and pay off in the morning. What shall I do?" The answer came back: "Lay the *Ruth* up."

In the same year that the fever raged there was unprecedented low water. The river shrank to a pathetic shadow of itself. An impudent wag at Keokuk announced that he had put on boots, boots that were not even hip boots, and had waded across the great Mississippi, the great Father of Waters, with dry feet. Such pleasantries, true or untrue, were not to the liking of river men. The times were too grim, calamity too heartbreaking in its inevitable succession. From Saint Paul to New Orleans half the proud packets of the Atlantic and Mississippi line were aground or laid up. Only boats of the lightest draught, and then with diminished cargoes, could find water enough in the stricken Mississippi. According to a newspaper of the day, "Boats drag their slow length along, and come when they get ready. A person to take passage on one would have to swing his hammock on the levee, and lay in a stock of crackers for fodder, for there is no telling when they will arrive."

In the general conspiracy there was nothing lacking — air, earth, and water arrayed against the difficult commerce of the Mississippi system. Or so it must have seemed to those who were trying to revive it. Bitter winters closed the river to navigation at Saint Louis and far below through stale, profitless weeks. Ice jams caught several defenseless boats and crushed their wooden hulls as though they had been paper-thin.

And as though these calamities had not been sufficient to defeat the ambitions of the men who had staked fortune and future on the river, there persisted the inner weaknesses of structure and organization — perhaps inevitable in the very nature of the business — that had been apparent even before the Civil War, with the encroachment of the railroads. It was painfully hard for the elephant to dance, for the lion to sing in chorus.

Irate shippers and passengers complained that the beautiful time schedules, patterned after railroad schedules, were for the most part only an amiable gesture of good will. Captains still suited their own convenience in departing and arriving. In the face of ever sharper competition the old Pittsburgh style of ringing departing bells one week in advance of the real time of departure was not practical. There was frank warning from friendly newspapers that this indolent, indifferent behavior had gone a long way to kill the trade on the Red River, the White River, the Arkansas, and now even the Missouri. Shippers along the Arkansas had hurried their shipments to the wharfboat and stowed them on board in response to the imperative "departing bells," only to watch a week slip by with the steamer still at the levee, waiting, perhaps, for a more profitable cargo.

Frequent rate wars, often growing out of the most childish antipathies and antagonisms between individual captains, resulted in disastrous entries in red ink in steamboat ledgers. The packets

Harry Johnson and *Tom Jasper* were having a "lively time," cutting rates in half and then cutting them again to get business away from each other. And what was most unfortunate, said a newspaper account of the private war between the *Harry Johnson* and the *Tom Jasper,* was the lower the rates went, the lower people thought they ought to go. One man shipped three cattle from Saint Paul to Saint Louis at the absurd rate of three dollars a head and then demanded free passage for himself since "it was the custom to 'pass' the man in charge of stock." Such were the vicissitudes of the rugged individualists who battled each other for the dying commerce of the Mississippi.

A constant warfare went on between owner, officers, and crew. Pilots at the close of the rebellion had tried desperately to hold wages to the old dizzy levels. For a brief time they hovered between five and eight hundred dollars a month and then, when it was apparent that good pilots were as plentiful as greenbacks, the whole wage scale underwent a drastic revision. By agreement among the several lines, the pilots' wages were cut to $200 a month, or $2,000 a year. This was a humiliation that the whole fraternity of the river seemed to share, a symbol of the passing of all that had been high, wide, and handsome. That first clerks, engineers, and mates were reduced to a meager $125, lamp trimmers and second stewards to $25, and cabin boys to $18 was nothing compared to the indignity put upon that lord of all creation, the pilot. He fought back, but in a desultory, hopeless way; shorn of the privileges and prerogatives of his position, he could no longer maintain his excesses, his extravagances, his wild flights of temperament, the untrammeled freedom of his art. And the final ignominy was the fact that under the new wage scale the captain was his equal. These wage cuts were part of a desperate effort to make a surplus that could go into dividends.

Improvements in steamboat construction were slow to be adopted, meeting indifference or stubborn prejudice. The iron hull was long agitated, and yet only a few boats of this construction were built prior to 1880. A lethargy, a pall, a great weariness hung over the river.

The Atlantic and Mississippi Steamship Company, which had begun so proudly, seemed about to collapse. In July of 1867 the boats of the line were advertised for sale at auction. A number of the more ardent officers and stockholders refused to surrender. They advanced the money necessary to save the line from bankruptcy.

Less than a year elapsed before bankruptcy again threatened. The ardor of the most ardent river men had now cooled. Many stockholders had lost considerable sums, small fortunes that represented the accumulation of a lifetime. The proud packets went under the hammer. "The *Mary E. Forsyth*, 255 feet long, 4 boilers, 25-inch cylinder engines, 8-foot stroke. The *Luminary*, 260 feet long . . . very fast boat. The *Julia* . . . hull good, good cabin and outfit. The *Mississippi* . . . wrought-iron shafts to work 16-foot bucket . . . fine cabin." So they were set down in the advertisement that consigned them to the block.

A much more modest line, the St. Louis and New Orleans Packet Company, came out of the ruin. And there were other lines that sought to conserve the trade of the river. But never again was there so bold and courageous an attempt to consolidate the dominion of the Mississippi, to confine the turbulent river and the wild, unruly commerce of the past within the pattern of a narrower, sharper era.

Now and then there was the brief illusion of the old, fierce, free life. When the packets that bore the great names — *Robert E. Lee, Natchez, Lady Gay* — raced up and down the river, with the people of the whole valley in one vast audience lined along the banks with flags flying and bands playing, then you could believe that the Mississippi system had indeed revived. But there was a great difference between such historic racing as that between the *Lee* and the *Natchez,* and the steamboat racing of the past. The former was a carefully engineered stunt, designed to draw the attention of the world, not racing for racing's sake as in the old days when pilot, passengers, and crew took part in impromptu trials with whatever boat might be encountered, risking lives and property at the drop of a hat, the whisper of a challenge. This new racing was safe, intended to get back the black headlines and public interest that it did get. What had been mortal combat became a polite exercise in swordsmanship — thrilling enough while it was going on, enlisting the most intense interest, but after all a stunt, carefully planned and shrewdly executed from beginning to end, serving briefly the purposes of publicity.

10

Jay Gould as River Man

The men of finance who had developed the railroads resolved to destroy once and for all the commerce of the river. With the end of the Civil War they began a campaign as ruthless as it was unrelenting. New lines were everywhere projected to parallel water routes. The directors of the Illinois Central built their line down the lower Mississippi valley to the very threshold of New Orleans. The Northwestern and the Rock Island were pushed out into Nebraska and the remoter West where once the Missouri River had been dominant. Several roads prepared to tap the province of the upper Mississippi; lines were planned to pass within the shadow of the high bluffs at the water's edge from Saint Paul southward.

It was a contest absurdly unequal. The ruin of the South was alone almost enough to destroy the trade of the river. The railroads had the heavy advantage of year-round operation, an advantage they were not slow to press. The new railroads approached the big shippers with offers of low uniform rates for their business through the entire year. When bad channels were added to the inevitable four or five months that the river was frozen, it was impossible to resist this offer.

Railroad rate structures were ingeniously designed with the sole purpose of taking trade from the packets. Special low rates, often below the cost of the haul, were offered to lure freight from the Mississippi. Inland towns, where the railroads had an unquestioned monopoly, paid through the nose to make up for these proffers of bait that were being constantly held out, but this was not too obvious.

Because the interests of the financiers who owned and directed the railroads interlocked with innumerable other enterprises in the expanding industrialism of the North and the Middle West, the railroads obtained privileges and rights denied to the steamboats. A law was passed forbidding riverboats to carry petroleum and the evidence seemed quite clear, to river men at least, that railroad interests were responsible for this restriction. In the spring of 1866 a delegation from Pittsburgh visited Washington to protest, forcing the secretary of the treasury to rule that the new law did not forbid the transportation by steamboat of "refined petroleum of not less than one hundred degrees Fahrenheit." Further, in response to the angry clamor of the steamboatmen, the secretary decided that crude petroleum could be transported in barges towed by passenger steamers.

A few river men understood that an entirely new method of river transportation was necessary to compete with the railroads. The packets were losing their passenger business at a rate so alarming that it was plain to shrewder minds that the day of the luxurious passenger boat, with freight an incidental source of revenue, was definitely over. It was possible, an argument went, to conserve the heavy freight to the river system by means of barges operated on efficient schedules. Impatient critics said that at least a hundred steamboats were obsolete and entirely outmoded and should be burned up.

"I think it is a miserable system of vessels," Henry T. Blow told a Senate investigating committee.

> They are unfitted to the navigation of the river and I think that from a few experiments sagacity ought to have followed the requirements of the times. The effect of combinations is to increase freights and to run off a class of people from the river that have not got the capital to compete with them. I can illustrate that so you can probably understand it. There has been at the Exchange [in Saint Louis] for the last eighteen months a model of a vessel that will carry freight at

three-fourths the rates these vessels have been carrying it at
and make money; but the capital is in the hands of men who
are not building vessels of this kind because of the fact that
they have so many of these old worn-out, miserable things
that form their capital stock, and they do not propose to inaugurate a competition which would be destructive to them.

There had been early attempts to establish a barge line that
would handle grain in bulk and through the shifting of individual barges give the same swift facility of transfer the railroads
offered. This was to avoid the costly exchange of grain in bags
from upper-river to lower-river boats at Saint Louis. In the
spring of 1866 the Mississippi Valley Transportation Company
was organizing its line, buying the first of several steam tugs that
were said to have sufficient power to push a half dozen or more
barges. It was reported that these tugs would be able to run for
one-half, or even less than half, the cost of operating the old-style
packet.

From the first, the Mississippi Valley Transportation Company had an alliance — how close was a matter of much speculation — with the railroads. The first president of the company,
Captain George H. Rea, had large railroad holdings which he
constantly increased, being at one time a director of the Missouri
Pacific line. This led to the suspicion that the barge line was
merely a device to serve the ulterior purpose of the railroads.

In the beginning years the barges were balked by the same obstacles that defeated the packets of the Atlantic and Mississippi
Steamship Company. The long drought and unprecedented low
stages of water in the late sixties were almost as disastrous to this
new method of freight transportation as to the passenger system.
In December of 1867 there were twenty boats aground in one
short stretch of the river below Cape Girardeau, most of them
towboats. Barges, many of them cut adrift, were hard aground
too. It was possible — just possible — to find three and a half
feet of water with the yawl, but for purposes of practical navigation, river captains swore, there was only three feet of water in
the channel.

And yet the line prospered, or at any rate it remained solvent. This was thanks, rumor had it, to railroad support. The roads, so the rumor went, wanted to foster and control what seemed likely to be the only profitable form of river transportation. Greater efficiency of operation, in loading, in transfer, in speed, made it seem inevitable that slow, heavy freight would be conserved to the barges of the river system for a long time to come. And yet with natural hazards and the pressure of new railroad lines springing up almost literally overnight, progress was slow enough.

River men still insisted, for all the success of the barge line, that the railroads' policy was rule and ruin. They thrust every obstacle they could into the channel of the Mississippi. Railroad bridges multiplied and, according to the river men, were always so located as to interfere with the movement of river traffic. Each collision was an occasion for a momentary burst of the old fury. Captain Able Hutchinson's steamboat, the *George I. Palmer,* was a victim of the "trap" that was the Quincy bridge, and Captain Hutchinson was served with notice, by the president of the bridge company, to remove the sunken wreck "as an obstruction to navigation." "A bridge company calling a sunken steamboat an obstruction to navigation certainly reminds one of the fable wherein a pot called the kettle black," was the response. The Northern Line packet *Dubuque* arrived in Saint Louis in "a sadly dilapidated state" as the result of a collision with that "universally execrated structure known as the Rock Island Bridge." Repairs would cost at least five thousand dollars. The bridge that had been just built between Fulton, Illinois, and Clinton, Iowa, was said to be "equally as bad."

"Everywhere in this valley," ran a resolution of the Mississippi Valley Commercial Convention at Keokuk, "railways owing their existence to land grants and right-of-way derived from the states, and money freely given by municipal corporations are using these franchises to prevent the producer from choosing his market and the consumer from obtaining his grain and meat at the least cost. They are used to break up the commerce of cities upon the river by local rates, charging us more upon freight from river cities to the interior than upon similar merchandise carried from distant eastern points."

The number of barges and steam towboats increased as they took more and more freight from the outmoded packets. More efficient and reliable, the barge line adopted modern devices, such as portable elevators, to meet railroad competition. But the gains that the barge lines made were virtually all at the expense of the packets. Total shipments by the Mississippi system were dwindling or at a standstill, while great new grain-growing areas were yielding enormous harvests, and consequently huge revenues, to the new railroad lines that served them.

In response to the repeated demands of the Valley, expressed in innumerable river conventions, Congress in 1875 accepted Captain Eads's plan to open the mouth of the Mississippi with a twenty-eight-foot channel that could be so maintained that large oceangoing boats might dock at the port of New Orleans. The river had been an almost landlocked lake, its mouth choked with the alluvial deposit of centuries. Now, said river men, it was an arm of the sea as far up as Saint Louis. For a brief time it appeared that the growing prophecies of revived trade to follow upon the opening of the jetties at the river's mouth would be fulfilled. In 1873 Saint Louis had shipped to New Orleans only 1,373,969 bushels of wheat and corn in bulk; in 1878, 5,451,603 bushels; in 1879, 6,164,838 bushels; and in 1880, after the completion of Captain Eads's jetties, 15,762,664 bushels.

So flourishing did this business appear that it attracted a man who had long been looked upon as the arch enemy of the river interests. Jay Gould's roving, voracious eye was not one to miss an opportunity for profit, wherever it might be. The river momentarily seemed to hold out renewed hope. Gould's Wabash Railroad system centered in Saint Louis, and he had only recently acquired the St. Louis, Iron Mountain and Southern, which gave him a direct route to New Orleans, Galveston, Mobile, and the whole Gulf of Mexico. Plainly the cheap water haul, while its promise of gain was negligible to such a titan of finance, offered a certain threat to the Gould railway system.

Gould acquired control of the St. Louis and New Orleans

Transportation Company, a barge line that had been started in competition with two earlier companies. This was mere child's play for the great financier who had scrambled and unscrambled half the railways of the country to his own enormous gain. When the foreign demand for grain fell off, as it did very shortly after the completion of the jetties, and barges lay idle at every wharf, only Gould's line could stand the strain. He absorbed his two competitors and reduced the name of the single line that now controlled all the freight traffic of the river, except the little that was left to the packets, to the St. Louis and Mississippi Valley Transportation Company.

Under the direction of a man so powerful this must mean the revival of the river, the hopeful said. In the East, too, they hoped that Gould's operations on the Mississippi might bring lowered freight rates, a naive hope, it would seem, from this perspective. "The cost of transportation to New Orleans is eight cents a bushel, just a quarter of the present railroad rates to Atlantic ports," said the *Philadelphia Press* approvingly. "Railroad pools cannot longer arbitrarily determine the price of our food. River competition means lower rates to tidewater and increased consumption of American grain in Europe." The *Jay Gould,* flagship of the line, had in one tow barges containing 231,000 bushels of bulk corn and 50,000 bushels of bulk wheat, eastern newspapers reported. What was more, weather would be no hindrance, for if the river at Saint Louis was frozen, as it was in severe winters, grain for export to Europe could be hauled by Jay Gould's railroad to Cairo and there be put onto barges.

But Gould, as the river advocates soon learned, was not a man to pursue modest returns through year-to-year endeavor. What actually happened is not known. There are several stories and all lead to the conclusion that Gould killed the line when it had served his purpose. One report is that Gould and the president of the company knew that it was making money but withheld this information from the other stockholders until together they had acquired most of the stock at a very low figure, realizing a neat profit while the foreign demand for grain persisted. And then the company was allowed to die. Another report is that Gould deliberately acquired control of all barges on the Mississippi, through one financial trick or another, to take them out of competition with his railroad to the Gulf. Those barges which he did not burn or junk he sold for use on the Ohio River, with the stipulation that they would not be returned to the Mississippi trade.

In a period of less than twenty years the river was all but swept bare. By 1887 there was only one regular steamboat line between Cincinnati and New Orleans. No boats ran from New Orleans to the Cumberland and Tennessee rivers, and there was no regular Louisville boat. As early as 1880 shipments of cotton from the Arkansas and the White rivers had virtually ceased. These had been among the most lucrative sources of steamboat income. The Red and the Ouachita still clung for a time to traffic that was too remote from a railway to be economically handled in that manner. But in 1881 a branch of the Texas and Pacific was completed that paralleled the Mississippi to Baton Rouge, and followed in general the direction of the Red River as far as Shreveport. This soon reduced the commerce of the Red River to insignificance. The trade of Vicksburg was entirely lost to New Orleans when the Yazoo and Mississippi Valley Railroad, running through the Mississippi delta region, was opened in 1884. New methods of purchasing, compressing, and shipping cotton also served to divert trade from the surviving packets to the railroads.

With the exception of Bayou Sara, not a single town on the lower Mississippi of over a thousand population was without a rail connection with New Orleans, Saint Louis, or Memphis by 1887. For the packets there was left only the local commerce between dwindling river villages and what captains could wheedle at larger ports. Humble suppliants now, captains begged, hat in hand, for what little freight was left over. In 1860, 27 percent of the total exports from the United States went by way of New Orleans, and 6.3 percent of the imports were received through this gateway; in 1886 this had been reduced to 12 percent and 1.1 percent; and in 1907 it would be 9.07 percent and 3.3 percent.

It was a fixed policy of the railroads to buy up all valuable terminal sites and in many instances they acquired holdings on the levees of river towns that were useful in throttling river competition. Towns on the upper Mississippi that had promised so much in the fifties were long since static or reduced to less than their flourishing beginnings. The census of 1900 would show only three towns — Quincy, Davenport and Dubuque — in the nine hundred miles between Saint Louis and Saint Paul with a population of more than twenty-five thousand.

Although the defeat of the river was certain from the beginning, it was not achieved without a long and painful conflict. In the course of that conflict it was inevitable that sectional antagonisms should be deepened, sectional jealousies accentuated. The masters of railroad finance proceeded to complete domination of the province of the Mississippi with utter disregard for what had been in the past. A deep-rooted sense of injustice was to take vague form, embodied in the never failing demand for river improvement — river improvement that should somehow restore the independence and autonomy of the past. The clamorous voice of the river was sometimes confused, but always it returned to this demand that the government should make up for the tribute that the men in the East who owned the railroads drew from the province of the West.

11

City Against City

Destiny hovered large over America with the swift expansion
that came at the war's end. And nowhere was it so manifest, so
splendid, as in those two great cities of the Middle West, Saint
Louis and Chicago. In their bitter rivalry they typified the con-
tending forces of river and railroad, the old West and the new.
Each was to be the metropolis of the midlands, of America, of
the world. Civic pride took this for granted in the city by the
river as well as in the city by the lake. The forces that would decide the fate of the two had long since been shaped, the end of
the race decreed. But with the burgeoning of a new boom, the
noisy clamor of new industries, the rise of new fortunes, there
were none to doubt, publicly at least, that growth must continue
by an inevitable process, geometric and astonishing, in Saint
Louis as in Chicago.

Saint Louis had the lead, a generous lead, it was thought. The
census of 1860, just before the outbreak of the rebellion, had
shown her with a population of 160,773, to Chicago's 109,250.
The latter had had an amazing growth during the war, but then
so had Saint Louis, and only ardent Chicagoans believed that the
race was really much closer than the census figures indicated.

Saint Louis was discovering that her river was, strangely
enough, a handicap. For so long it had been a natural advantage,
bearing each year a greater tide of immigration and commerce,
that it was difficult or impossible to face such an unpleasant fact.
But this natural advantage had been made to yield handsome

profits to a few men, and these profits had been the basis of a monopoly that had flung a ring as of steel about the city. The river was now a water hurdle, and a fearfully broad and deep one, in the race for supremacy. Those who believed in the city's growth and expansion with all the ardor of Chicago's boosters fought and fought and fought again, for years without avail, to break the monopoly that had entrenched itself upon the banks of the Mississippi. Chicago was, in contrast, young, free, unhampered by the past.

The Wiggins Ferry Company is a classic example of a monopoly built upon a simple human necessity. Wily Samuel Wiggins got from the General Assembly of Illinois on March 2, 1819 a franchise that gave him a clear monopoly for ferrying on the Illinois shore opposite Saint Louis. Before the city of East Saint Louis was even thought of, Samuel Wiggins had put a fence around it. Mr. Wiggins, shrewd Yankee that he was, absorbed his two competitors and sat down on the riverbank to grow rich. People had to cross the Mississippi to get to the rising young town of Saint Louis, and for this privilege they paid Mr. Wiggins and paid him very well. Within twelve years Mr. Wiggins's tight little monopoly had become such a good thing that he was offered a handsome sum to sell out to a syndicate of leading citizens, among them his son William. Thus the Wiggins Ferry Company was born.

With each westward immigrant, with each nutmeg and spool of thread that crossed the river, the Wiggins Ferry Company grew richer. And as its capital grew so did its hold upon the young city, for capital went inevitably into depots, yards, boats, warehouses. Charters and franchises expired and were renewed by compliant legislatures. The Wiggins Ferry Company knew well how to arrange those matters. Saint Louis passed ordinances intended to permit competing ferry lines, but the Wiggins Ferry Company took care that there should be only enough competition to quiet the public's apprehension, which was in actuality no competition at all.

When the railroads reached the Mississippi opposite Saint Louis, there was the Wiggins Ferry Company, willing and eager to serve. In fact, if a railroad so much as hinted that it might like to enter Saint Louis another way, the Wiggins Ferry suggested, gently but firmly, that it would be better to come along with good old Wiggins after all. And most railroads saw the light of reason. When they didn't, they got into lawsuits that were costly, never-ending, and rarely successful. With the railroads came even greater prosperity. Each car that crossed the river paid tribute to Wiggins. Great new car ferries were built, switching lines and freight terminals.

While occasional legal skirmishes were lost, the Wiggins Ferry Company had built its monopoly in steel and stone along both banks of the river. It seemed more enduring than the earth itself. People complained that the ferries were dark and ill-kept, the wharfboats were uncovered and passengers were compelled to stand out in the open under the blazing sun of summer or the biting, damp cold of winter. Saint Louis and East Saint Louis tried in vain to collect more taxes from the "Old Reliable." Low water, high water, and floating ice often delayed or interrupted service. Boiler explosions fed the resentment that had begun to grow. Popular indignation mounted. And the Wiggins Ferry Company grew richer and richer.

But with the close of the war the champions of a bridge began to gather strength. It was the essence of Saint Louis's dream of progress and achievement, the bridge that should leap over the obstacle to east and west travel. Opposed to the bridge were all the forces of monopoly and special privilege that had been attached to the river system.

The land needed for the approaches on the Illinois side was owned, of course, by the Wiggins Ferry Company, and at first "Old Reliable," a name given half in affection, half in contempt, declined to yield a single inch of it. Forced by pressure of the law and public opinion to surrender, "Old Reliable" held out for a price of $150,000 for a tract that a commission had appraised at $97,000 and for which the bridge company offered $25,000. There was a wearisome legal dispute that went from court to court before a compromise was reached.

The dwindling steamboat interests promptly took their case to

Washington and enlisted the aid of those ultimate guardians of the Mississippi, the United States Corps of Engineers. In their report, the engineers found numerous faults with the plans for the bridge that Engineer James B. Eads was pushing with the skill and forthrightness that characterized everything he did. A horizontal bridge twenty-seven feet higher than the one Eads projected was what steamboatmen demanded. "Which is equivalent," said a newspaper of the time, "to saying that nothing short of no bridge at all will be entirely satisfactory to the few steamboats that claim a monopoly of the river, from its bed below to the clouds above."

The engineers took up half of their report with scientific arguments to prove that the towering chimneys of the *James Howard*, which would reach ten feet above the horizontal trusses of the bridge in low water, could not be made a foot lower without impairing the draft. Angrily the champions of the bridge replied that since the *James Howard* was a lower-river boat she probably never had gone above the location of the bridge and probably never would have occasion to go above it. If the *James Howard* should choose to go above Saint Louis and the river should be at flood stage, it was pointed out, the bridge, to accommodate it, would have to be a hundred and six feet above the water — sixty-three feet higher than the bridge that Eads planned. "No matter how high in the air a bridge may be suspended," said an advocate of the Eads plan, "a steamboat owner has only to run his chimneys above it to make it an 'obstruction to navigation' and secure a report from a government commission in favor of its destruction."

It was not only in Saint Louis that the river interests struggled to preserve the profits and prerogatives of a dying order. At New Orleans the Towboat Company and the "canal ring" levied tribute on all boats that passed out of the mouth of the Mississippi to the sea. For unless they were of the lightest draught they had to be pushed over the bars that blocked the river's mouth. It was a monopoly as complete, as rock-ribbed as the one that Samuel Wiggins had established at Saint Louis.

And when Captain Eads, having begun his bridge, came down

to offer a plan to dredge out the Mississippi's mouth, the Towboat Company fought him with the same tireless energy that the Wiggins Ferry Company had displayed. It was too good a thing to surrender, this barrier of mud that enabled the company to exact its inevitable toll. Advocates of the river system raised an angry clamor against the Towboat Company, but it persisted in blocking the mouth of the Mississippi until the last legal recourse was exhausted. "What right has any individual, corporation, or ring to stand at your gate and make an unreasonable charge for pulling you over when you may open it and walk in and out without cost?" The answer lay in the entrenched capital that the monopoly had accumulated through the years when the river system flourished undisturbed by competition. "The Towboat Company and canal ring evidently believe Captain Eads' plan will prove successful and thereby destroy the bright hopes of those who are feathering their nests at the expense of the Mississippi Valley."

Shippers along the Missouri River claimed that a steamboat monopoly was charging exorbitant rates, with the result that as fast as railroads were built grain was being diverted from Saint Louis to Chicago. From points along the Missouri in southern Nebraska it was cheaper by ten cents per hundred pounds to ship by rail to Chicago rather than by water to Saint Louis. "If this be the boasted competition between river and rail carriage, another river would certainly lay Saint Louis in the shade," said the Brownsville, Nebraska *Advertiser* in 1870. "This is not the real trouble; the trouble is Chicagoans feel an individual responsibility in building up Chicago, while St. Louisans feel immediately for self, and such monopolists as now have hold of the steamboat interests are allowed to grind shippers along the Missouri to the immense damage of the grain and mercantile interests of that city."

In defense, Saint Louis said that responsibility for high rates lay largely with the towns along the rivers. Each one felt privileged to tax the steamboat trade to the limit. Besides ordinary property taxes, there were wharfage charges, inspection fees, license fees, stamp duties. Hull insurance on the Missouri cost 11 to 13 percent of the cost of the boat. With these burdens and the difficulties of navigation, the so-called steamboat monopolies had no profits to show for their pains.

In Chicago there were no monopolies of government or business surviving from the slowly dying past to block the way. Capitalists from the East, such as Mayor William Butler Ogden, later to be the first president of the Union Pacific Railroad, had an absolutely free hand to do what they would with their capital. Railroads multiplied as if by magic. Chicago wholesale houses extended their territory even farther and farther.

In view of Chicago's amazing growth and the fundamental differences that set the two cities apart, it is extraordinary that Saint Louis could continue to believe in her own supremacy. Yet there seem to have been no skeptics in the destiny chorus, not even small doubts of the inevitability of growth at an undiminished pace. If Chicago had "Deacon" Bross, Saint Louis had Logan Uriah Reavis. They were both crackbrained, obsessed with illusions of grandeur, of marble cities that should rise from the squalid mud of lake and river front.

Coming from the bottoms of the Sangamon River, the country of Abraham Lincoln, Reavis adopted Saint Louis with the fervor of a prophet. His first pamphlet, *The New Republic,* published in 1867, was already attuned to grandiose prediction. Two years later he brought out the more spectacular *Removal of the National Capital from the Atlantic Seaboard to the Valley of the Mississippi* — specifically, to Saint Louis. This was not a dream, nor a hope, but an eventuality which the prophet promised would come to pass. Between 1867 and 1870 he wrote five more pamphlets, all intended "to show the glory and greatness of Saint Louis, and of the Mississippi basin." And while elsewhere, especially in Chicago, they laughed at Saint Louis's "colossal Capital-mover," the city of his adoption bought no less than a hundred and fifty thousand copies of his writings. They fed Saint Louis's secret illusions, silenced all doubt.

The most absurd jealousies existed between the two rivals. Saint Louis accused Chicago of trying to obstruct plans for the bridge through the insidious plot of one L. B. Boomer. Mr.

Boomer came from Chicago and incorporated as the St. Louis
and Illinois Bridge Company. Inasmuch as the name of Eads's
concern was the Illinois and St. Louis Bridge Company, there
may have been grounds for suspecting Mr. Boomer's motives.
But even if he had been burning with a desire to bridge the Mississippi, the very fact that he was from Chicago would have
damned his project in the public eye.

"It is a most astonishing thing that the people of St. Louis will
stand still and see themselves robbed of all the fruit that is to
come from this enterprise," Henry Blow thundered out at a
meeting of the St. Louis Board of Trade, "by an overgrown and
voracious rival city; a city that sends a man here for the purpose
of prostrating this very enterprise; a city, sir, that is willing, as
one of these gentlemen said in my presence, to pay a quarter of a
million dollars to the representatives of a rival enterprise if by
that means they could postpone the building of the bridge five or
six years."

Mr. Boomer withdrew from the field and Eads absorbed his
company, but there were other disputes to whip on the jealousy
between the two now bitter enemies. Chicago boasted that a report on the Chicago school system had taken 318 pages and had
cost $4,500 while a similar report on the Saint Louis school sys-
tem had been concluded in 32 pages and had cost only $150.
When Chicago pointed to its rare charms as a summer resort,
Saint Louis sneered and said, yes, and how summer visitors
would enjoy the stench from the open stream that carried off the
city's sewage. Saint Louis claimed that it cost only forty cents a
bushel to send corn from Saint Paul to Liverpool by way of New
Orleans, while it cost sixty-four cents from Saint Paul via Chicago, the Lakes, Buffalo, and New York. And Chicago answered
that grain shipped by the Gulf suffered marked deterioration in
the hot, humid air of that region.

The results of the census of 1870 were awaited with an eagerness and tension such as might hinge upon the outcome of a battle. It showed that Saint Louis had a population of 310,864; Chicago, 298,977. Bonfires were lit in the streets of the river city
while Chicago cried fraud. The census takers had counted the

dogs and the first settlers in Bellefontaine Cemetery, said Chicago. But the margin was so narrow that Saint Louis had no enduring assurance from this triumph.

In the city by the Mississippi there was an undercurrent of doubt that showed itself in a heightened sensitivity to criticisms from the city by the lake. When the compiler of a business yearbook gave Chicago a slight edge over Saint Louis at the beginning of 1871, Saint Louis heaped abuse and ridicule upon him. He was caricatured in the newspapers and his findings were pronounced a tissue of prejudice and injustice.

And when in the spring of 1871, the great fire ravaged Chicago, the lamentations heard in Saint Louis were not unmixed with a kind of smug self-righteousness. It was, Saint Louis felt, the verdict of a just God upon a brash upstart. All day long people stood in the streets before the bulletin boards as the telegraph disclosed the magnitude of the catastrophe. Fire that leaped like wind across the grass. Fleeing multitudes. Fireproof buildings burned like tinder. No hope for Chicago. The city destroyed. A curious silence hung over the crowds that watched in the Saint Louis streets. There was the prophet, Reavis — slightly hunchbacked and hip-shot, the light of a suppressed eagerness on his grotesque, furrowed face — never moving from the bulletin board, as the messages of disaster were frequently changed, mopping at himself with his big filthy bandana handkerchief. He would not speak one word, he was too kind-hearted to exult openly over the misfortune even of an enemy. "Still," as a local historian wrote, "when the other men would crack a hideous joke over Chicago's new business triumph as a crematory, he could not help wheezing out one of his huge-chested guffaws which would wind up in a prolonged laughing cough." And as he walked away he was heard to say, "I told you so. The Lord is on the side of Saint Louis."

For seven years the bridge had been in progress, and at last with all obstacles, physical and financial, behind, it was completed in 1874. This, many believed, was to usher in the millennium. But disillusionment was not long in coming. The Wiggins Ferry Company began a campaign of savage competition, mercilessly undercutting rates with the aid of capital reserves built up through long years of monopoly. The bridge had cost — including damages, commissions, and numerous unexpected expenses — approximately $10 million, which was more than twice the original estimate, and the bonds were soon in default. But even worse, the businessmen who had clamored most loudly for a bridge did not hesitate to take advantage of the ferry's competitive rates. For nearly a year after its construction little or no traffic passed over Captain Eads's beautiful bridge. While it was indeed very handsome and was reputed to be a triumph of certain engineering principles, it had not, after all, been built as a monument. Soon it was necessary to compromise with the "Old Reliable." The monopoly that shrewd Samuel Wiggins had staked out in 1819, was unbeatable. It retained its hold upon the city, squeezing it and pinching it and strangling it, through the era of great industrial expansion and down almost to the present time.

In everything, and above all in their physical appearances, the two cities were antithetical. Saint Louis was beginning to show the first signs of age, Chicago seemed to be forever bursting out of bounds like a crude young giant. With age there had come to Saint Louis a kind of dignity, a neoclassic grace. Lucas Place was a street of handsome town houses that might have adorned Boston or London. Under an archway of old trees carriages with footmen passed, bearing ladies to their afternoon calls.

A society that assumed the prerogatives of a minor aristocracy had come into vague being. You were descended from one of the early voyageurs who founded the city, you belonged to the proper clubs, you lived in Lucas Place, or you did not. There were "gentlemen," skilled in the making of punches and juleps, in arranging cotillions, and in directing the affairs of their conservative banking houses. "Culture" of a sort was at least tolerated in the community, and even a philosophical movement, an attenuated Hegelism, flourished briefly. A superior brothel admitted to its carefully guarded portals only the most correct dandies and aging bucks. If all this existed like a beleaguered island in the vast sea of immigration that had fairly overwhelmed the old city, it nevertheless did exist.

Chicago began all over again, the prairie swept clean by fire. What had seemed a calamity was in reality a gift of the gods. While the ruins of the city still smouldered, Chicago's boosters had gone East to persuade new capital to build Chicago over again. And it came in a golden flood, with all the rich rewards of expansion, expansion in every direction and in every field; it was the pioneer epoch over again but on an incredibly vast scale. Chicago was as raw and violent as a mining camp, with the same swift shifting of fortunes, and the same tension and hope.

To Saint Louis the census of 1880 came like a clap of thunder, shattering the comforting illusion of two decades. The records stood: Chicago, 503,185; Saint Louis, 350,518. Saint Louis appointed her principal mathematician and a staff of assistants to prove that the city by the lake had padded the returns, but this was a futile endeavor. Chicago had won, and what was most galling to Saint Louis was Chicago's indifference since she had long before been confident of this triumph. The city by the river was no longer even considered a rival. The sharp disillusion that Saint Louis felt persisted for many years, a discontent that was a part of the atmosphere of defeat and frustration that hung like a mist over the river, over the whole valley.

12

To the North

If the great tidal wave of energy that peopled the lower valley
had spent itself, there was just beginning to the north an epoch in
which giants would again walk the earth and conquer the rivers,
men of legendary strength not unlike the boatmen of a much
earlier day. Along the upper reaches of the Mississippi and its
tributaries in Wisconsin and Minnesota were great forests of timber, far richer and more accessible than those that were on the
verge of exhaustion in the East. Up to the period of the Civil War
these forests had lain like a buried Golconda; only the outermost
limits were scratched by remote settlers and roving timber
thieves.

But the towns along the upper Mississippi multiplied their
populations again and again after the war, and all the vast, tree-
less prairie to the west was filling up. The newcomers would not
be content for long with sod huts, with makeshift dwellings; they
would want lumber for houses and barns and hog pens, for side-
walks and new steamboats, for railroad ties and fine new wagons.
The forests to the north were inexhaustible; so everyone believed. And the river was a broad, free highway between these
remote forests and the vast prairie. Soon after the war had ended,
the realization grew in the minds of a few sharp men that here
was a prize to be had for the taking, and what a prize it was for
the men of force, the men of iron will, the men of indomitable
strength and consummate shrewdness. There began such a pillage as has rarely been seen.

Up to as late as 1870 the whole process was leisurely. Rafts, either of logs or of lumber sawed in small mills in the pineries, were floated down the Mississippi to markets as far south as Saint Louis. It took such a raft — rarely more than four hundred feet long — from twelve to sixteen days to float downstream. For long interludes, in open stretches of the river, the crews enjoyed a lusty leisure. If the night threatened to be dark, with possible storms, the raft put in at a familiar island, where more often than not a rustic house of pleasure was to be found. There, captain, pilots, and roosters (which was river for roustabout) caroused and square danced, wenches in gay calico would be swung clear off the floor by raftsmen who towered above six feet almost without exception.

In the days of the floating rafts the roosters were a proud lot. They were fellows of Paul Bunyan, French Canadians many of whom elected, when the drive of logs ended in the spring, to spend the summer rafting. Others had come from the thinning forests of New Brunswick, Maine and Pennsylvania, experienced log drivers of tough Scotch and Irish stock. When the wind was high or the current swift, they sweated at the great sweeps that were fixed at bow and stern. Each man raised his oar from the water, walked with it a short distance, then let it down and threw his whole weight against it. In stormy weather they worked hours on end, lashed by rain and wind.

Other rafts were steered by "tamaracking." A half dozen of the crew worked at the huge sweep, made from a tamarack tree and fitted with a wide blade. They sang in unison as they carried it along and then pushed it back through the stiff current of the river. If it was a lumber raft, the men had a snug, sizeable house built for cooking and shelter; but on a raft of logs, the cook house was a crude hutch that provided little protection. It was whiskey that kept them strong, the raftsmen said.

Having floated down to the mill, the roosters were sent back up the river on a packet to bring down another raft. They traveled, of course, as deck passengers and under the ready impetus of cheap liquor they often made travel hideous for the more fastidious passengers who occupied the cabins on the upper decks.

They brawled and shouted and sang bawdy songs. At least once they mutinied.

The Northern Line steamer *Dubuque* was bound for Saint Paul. At Quincy, Illinois and again at Davenport, Iowa several hundred deck passengers were taken on board, roosters for the most part, with a few harvest hands. The trouble started when the clerk came down to collect fares, leaving a black deckhand armed with a club to watch the stairway. The guard was more or less traditional. What the roosters objected to was the club. One of the stoutest of the lot engaged the guard in a fight and was knocked prone on the deck for his pains. A free-for-all followed. The roosters swarmed over the boat; chairs, knives, axes flew through the air. At least a dozen blacks were killed outright. Others were shot and bludgeoned as they tried to swim away from the boat. The terrified officers, beleaguered on the upper deck, succeeded in getting a message ashore. At Clinton a force of several hundred armed citizens came out to take over the *Dubuque* and the roosters surrendered, many of them escaping ignominiously over the rail.

The shrewd adventurers, the Irish immigrants and the Yankee traders, were not long in improving this leisurely method of rafting. A way of rigging a raft was devised whereby a small steamboat could be employed to "tow," which meant to push, the raft downstream. The pace was enormously speeded up. Rafts increased in size until they were measured not by feet but by acres. Electric searchlights replaced the old pine-knot torches. When a raft neared completion the foreman of the drive would wire the officials of the mill and at once a steamboat would be sent for it. As the boat approached, the captain singled out and drew alongside the raft he was to take down the river. One by one, at their appointed places, the roosters dropped off to fix the lines and tighten the numerous strings, or ranks, into one stout whole, so that by the time the steamer had maneuvered into position the enormous mass of logs might be got in motion.

As often as not this process went forward at night under the glare of searchlights, and if a careless rooster missed his footing and slipped under the shifting mass of logs, he was lost. Many men were drowned in this way, but then, men were plentiful. Surefootedness and certain simple but precise skills were required of the roosters. The great burden rested on the captain. In the boom that was just beginning he usually owned his boat. He made contacts with the mills to bring rafts down the river and he was responsible for exactly so many thousand feet of logs. It was no simple task to shepherd this great unwieldy tow, valued at from $25,000 to $40,000, down a tortuous, troubled river.

These captains were stern, harsh men, bent on wresting their share of gain from the great potential wealth of the forests. They drove their crews to the limit of human endurance and set the same mark for themselves. Often in an entire summer they got not one whole night's sleep. They had to combat the fog that creeps out of the coulees that gash the high, palisaded banks of the upper river. They had to feel their way almost by instinct, with always the fear that the cargo they pushed before them might split up on some bar or shoal. Lake Pepin, formed by the widening of the Mississippi about half way between Saint Paul and Winona, Minnesota, was an unfailing source of danger. This lake, twenty-two miles long and two miles wide on the average, is subject to violent and sudden storms. Within a few minutes its whole surface may be lashed by waves twenty and twenty-five feet high. A raft wracked by such a storm could not long survive. In its blind, furious pitching it might sink the small boat that was attempting to hold it to a course. Early evening was said to be the most advantageous time to navigate Lake Pepin. There was hardly a captain who had not lost logs in the lake, logs to the value of five thousand or ten thousand dollars. And those were bitter losses, wrung from hard-gotten gains.

Most of the captains were Yankees from New England or northern New York. Stephen B. Hanks, Abraham Lincoln's cousin, was a captain to the very end, first of a floating raft and then of a steamboat in the rafting trade. There were names such as Hollinshead, Duncan, Fuller, Whistler, Savage, Reed, and Newcomb. And there were occasional Gallaghers and McCartys. For all the risks they ran, these hard-bitten men made money, and kept it, too.

Money was in the very air for those who were clever enough to grasp it. There were men who could look at a forest and tell to the dollar what it was worth at the mill. And these keen men, under the direction of the German peasant Frederick Weyerhaeuser, who had started out tending furnace in a sawmill at Rock Island, began to accumulate vast tracts of timber. Their early gains they put back into timber, always timber and more timber. There were many ways, besides purchase, of acquiring the "inexhaustible" stands of pine. No one cared what happened. The timber was inexhaustible, wasn't it? There were big poachers and little poachers and medium-size poachers, and government agents who grabbed great tracts for themselves.

As early as 1860 timber thefts had become general and flagrant in Wisconsin and Minnesota. "Numerous lumbering camps," said the Wisconsin commissioners of school lands, "are located on the best pine lands of the state, by companies of men who pretend to no shadow of title or authority, who get out logs for sale or on contract with mill owners, and shingles for market. Remoteness from the settlements had generally screened these camps from observation and the depredations committed from detection. So operations of this kind have gone on from year to year unmolested." Laws passed a few years later made some difference — it was possible for officers of the law to seize stolen timber if they could find it before it was floated away.

There were more subtle means of acquiring stands of pine. One was by taking up "soldiers' additionals," tracts granted to men who had served in the Civil War. A "soldier's additional" was a faded slip of paper in a forgotten drawer. When a soldier died his widow took a few dollars in cash for that slip of paper. Weyerhaeuser's Mississippi Logging Company accumulated thousands of these slips of paper; one block was worth "$400,000, more or less" — so Weyerhaeuser's attorney casually appraised its value. One may be sure that it was worth more before the forest was cut down.

But this was picayune, trivial, in comparison with the grants that certain adventurers took for themselves. There was one such grant that extended across the forest lands of an entire corner of the state of Wisconsin for a railway from a point on the Saint Croix River to the west end of Lake Superior. This contained an estimated 1,288,208 acres of forest land. Another grant through the Wisconsin forest was nearly as large. Men who made their start on the upper Mississippi were later to seize for themselves that vast prize, that great swath out of America's Northwest, the amazing grant to the Northern Pacific of 43,159,428 acres. It is no wonder a kind of folklore grew up that has persisted to the present day. The legend went that a government grant a hundred miles long had gone to one of the forest freebooters for a road through public lands into privately owned stands of timber. The width of the road was not specified and so it was cut a mile, two miles, three miles wide — the width depending on where the story was told — through the government's finest timber.

The incredible era of grab was nowhere so well exemplified as in these remote forests of the upper river. Bold theft was varied with every kind of shady practice.

> The difficulty was increased by the unscrupulousness of the recorders employed by the Federal government. It was the rule rather than the exception that the explorer who had undergone privation and hardship to find the timber, when he came to enter it at the land office, was met with the statement of the recorder that it had already been entered. This, of course, was not true. The recorder had a list of willing 'dummies' always at hand who were put down as the purchasers of property which was afterwards sold at a near profit to himself and his co-conspirators who supplied the money. The foundations of not a few American fortunes were laid in this reprehensible fashion.

Through a joker slipped into a bill in the Wisconsin legislature granting a gas franchise to the town of Portage, Weyerhaeuser's group gained control of advantageous rafting grounds at Beef Slough. Elaborate equipment was built to handle their logs as they came pouring down out of the Chippewa River in a great brown carpet that covered the whole stream. In 1868 there were rafted at Beef Slough 12,000,000 feet of logs. By 1873 this had increased to 274,367,900 feet. In the same year 195,398,830 feet of logs came down out of the Black River. The panic that struck that year caused a severe break in lumber prices but the boom hardly abated; there were seventy-three steamboats towing lumber on the upper Mississippi in the panic year.

One dominant desire persisted and that was to convert the forests into money as fast as possible. When the Wisconsin Railroad Commission succeeded in getting through the legislature a law that was, in effect, a tax on each of the logs that comprised a raft, drastic measures were necessary. The state had long looked with concern on the great wealth that was being stripped from its lands to flow down the Mississippi to the mills, there to be minted into gold. But the lumbermen were just as determined not to pay tribute to Wisconsin. Across the river from Beef Slough in Wisconsin was West Newton in Minnesota.

It was soon discovered that Minnesota was more tractable. In fact, it was found possible to elect a governor of that state who held a most tender regard for the lumber interests. He saw to it that certain necessary laws were put through the legislature. It only remained then to drive the logs across the Mississippi and form them into rafts at West Newton in order to escape the Wisconsin levy. To accomplish this a boom, that is, an arrangement of logging chains and logs, was stretched across the entire river. Boats going up or down had to whistle, as for a drawbridge, in order that a section of the boom might be momentarily opened.

Several times rival gangs fought with clubs and even guns over a strategic site for a boom. There was no code, no law; neither hell nor high water, certainly no consideration of decency or order, in any way restrained the ruthless men who were behind the drive. "The work of improvement of the river has been confined to points between Minneapolis and St. Cloud, where the worst obstructions existed, and, no doubt, some benefit to log driving has accrued," said an engineer's report for 1879. "The loggers, however, tear out the dams in order to obtain shorter routes through the chutes for the passage of logs. It has been impossible thus far to detect the depredators." Nor would the depredators be detected. Those who might have detected them were too preoccupied with making their own fortunes.

All down the Mississippi to Saint Louis there was a vast hum and stir. From Clinton, Burlington, Rock Island, La Crosse, and a half dozen other towns where east-to-west railways crossed the river, hundreds of carloads of lumber daily went westward. It was used prodigally. White pine that today would go into the finish of a fine interior was put into hog pens and cow barns. While the shrewder ones may have foreseen the end, the illusion of the inexhaustible pineries persisted.

Merchants and traders in the towns along the river believed their prosperity would continue forever. The saloons — and there were hundreds of them — did a booming business. It was customary, as a raft approached a town, for two or three roosters to put out in a Quincy skiff and row as rapidly as possible to the nearest saloon on the waterfront. Here they would put away a few drinks, buy as many jugs of whiskey as they could carry and then, by hard pulling, catch up with the raft again.

Although the roosters, who literally roosted wherever they could find a place to lay their heads, were driven ever harder and harder, they were far from being tamed. After the payoff when the raft was delivered, they would make the rounds of the saloons until their money gave out. They knew every jail and every sheriff along the route and they knew what towns to avoid. They fought and brawled and worked, all with an indiscriminate ardor. At the close of the rafting season in the late fall, if they did not choose to go into the logging camps for the winter, they would make their way by devious and uncertain routes to the deep South, where they would work in the cane fields during the winter. In late March they would begin to reappear, battered and frozen looking, eager for work to begin.

Up and down the river the glinting saws flashed, sawdust piles grew larger and larger, and still the logs came. The rafts continued to grow in size until it seemed that it would be humanly impossible to guide them down the river. The record lumber raft, so far as can be determined, consisted of sixteen strings, forty-four cribs long; it covered a space 270 feet by 1450 feet, or virtually nine acres — more than 9,000,000 feet of lumber. The largest log raft is said to have contained about 2,000,000 feet; it was 270 feet wide and 1,550 feet long.

The boom came to an end with the same dramatic suddenness that it had begun, and for a very good reason. There were no more logs. What was said to have been the largest sawmill in the world was built at Clinton in the nineties. After two years it was forced to close down. The vast forests of the North had in a space of twenty years been felled and swept down the stream in a movement without parallel for rapacity, for sheer force, in the world's history. The scope of this movement is difficult, if not impossible, to comprehend. Figures are to a certain degree meaningless, but they give some idea of what happened. Along the Mississippi and its tributaries above the Falls of Saint Anthony between the years 1848 and 1918 a total of 19,784,277,656 feet of lumber was cut. And the cutting below was far, far greater, the Chippewa valley yielding perhaps the greatest wealth of any of the forested river valleys.

A great, barren waste of cut-over country was left. Logging operations had been ruthless and crude, and fire inevitably followed in the wake of the logger. It was said in 1898 that nearly half of the forest area of the upper Mississippi had been burned over at least once. According to one state forestry report, "about three million acres are without any forest cover whatever and several million acres more are but partly covered by the dead and dying remnants of the former forest." This was what was left of the great wealth that had extended from Michigan through Wisconsin into Minnesota, covering the entire surface of twenty-seven counties in Wisconsin. According to one estimate, sixty-six billion feet of pine were cut in the latter state alone.

And yet the thefts continued. The few thousand acres that state and federal governments had been able to preserve from the general debacle were constantly assaulted. "For many years," said the state forester of Wisconsin in 1906, "timber trespass or the stealing of timber had been treated most leniently and in Wisconsin both the government and the state have suffered enormous losses in this way, so much so that it is exceptional to find a forty owned by either, which has not been trespassed upon and frequently every stick of merchantable timber has been cut." With the scarcity of first-stand timber the large lumber companies encouraged poor settlers to cut from the public lands, and to restrict this, at least in part, it was found necessary to pass a law making the buyer of stolen timber equally guilty with the thief. As late as 1897 it was found that one company had stolen nearly five million feet of pine and other valuable timber from swamplands of the Lac du Flambeau Indian Reservation. The contracting firm had represented to the secretary of the interior that the cutting was for the improvement of various buildings on the reservation.

What is most ironic is that according to the best estimates not more than 40 percent of the forest ever reached the sawmill. The rest was sacrificed to careless logging and fire. The cut-over country, poorly adapted to a precarious kind of agriculture, would forever after be a drain upon the states. As for the lumber barons, they took their profits and their experience and sought out new forests in the South and the Pacific Northwest. The German peasant Frederick Weyerhaeuser, who had begun with the shirt that he wore on his back, became a power in banks and railroads and shipping companies all through the Northwest.

It was in the American tradition: they came, they saw, they grabbed. How profoundly the pillage of these forests has affected the life of the great valley, we have only now begun to understand. Floods and fires, the earth itself, and the water under the earth have a relation to the behavior of those freebooters of the closing decades of the last century. It is above all in the towns along the river that one is aware of their impact and of the vast forces that they typified, aware of it if only in the quietude, the slow stagnation that has settled along the upper reaches of the river.

13

River Town

The anatomy of a river town is curiously revealing of what has happened along the Mississippi. A different kind of town, only by an accident of geography in Iowa or Illinois or Wisconsin, a river town had none of the blighting respectability of the traditional Main Street. It is far more highly colored; even in its present eclipse, it reflects the glow of a richer, gaudier past. Out of the very rise and fall of the river has come a special quality.

Many of the upper river towns that flourished in the days of the lumber boom have disappeared altogether, visible, if at all, as moldering ghost towns not unlike the ruins of the silver cities of Nevada. Others are dying, shrinking slowly into a pale semblance of the past. Galena is shut off from the Mississippi, its tributary, Fever River, choked with sand. Bad Axe in Wisconsin has become the somnolent village of Genoa. Dubuque dwindles and so do the other Iowa river towns — Clinton, Burlington, Muscatine. Beef Slough, once the center of tempestuous life, with a hundred rafting crews charging in and out of saloon and brothel, has vanished. So has West Newton, across the river.

Winslow is a town such as Clinton or Dubuque. It is in Iowa, but it has no more to do with that rural and circumspect state than has Vladivostock. In the beginning Joshua Winslow, a frostbitten Yankee from northern New York, came with his ailing wife and built a house on a rise of ground where the river was open, free from sandbars and towheads. That was in 1836. Slowly a town accumulated around the Winslows and their ofspring. Long before the Civil War, Joshua and his wife had died of the ague and chills and fever that attended upon early settlement in the valley.

Winslow in 1865, was a thriving town with more than three thousand inhabitants. It had eighty-six saloons and a subscription library. The Winslow Young Men's Association, which fostered the library, organized in that year a lecture series and brought to the town Emerson, Horace Greeley, P. T. Barnum, the freed slave Frederick Douglass, and two or three others of almost equal note. The association also gave a Promenade Festival at which the sum of $342 was raised to buy books. One of the local wits offered a humorous monologue in the person of "Professor A-gas-sick" of "Cambrick University," discoursing on Adam and Eve and the revised story of the Garden.

Already there were a half dozen sawmills at Winslow. In that year old Rizen Abbott paid a war tax to the government on ten thousand dollars of his income, and J. L. Westbrook is shown in the published lists with almost as much. But they were still amateurs, buying the logs they sawed in their mills from timber contractors in the pineries to the north or from chance raftsmen who came drifting down the stream to barter logs. But Abbott, Westbrook, and the Devines were soon to realize how kind God had been in joining the pineries to the prairie with the river.

Winslow was to become a sawdust town, a term of contempt as used by jealous landsmen from the interior. In the spring when the river opened and the first rafts came down the muddied, drift-laden flood to Winslow, the great circular saws set up their familiar shrieking whine again — the sawmill sound that carried so far on still, hot days in the summer. The shift was twelve to fourteen hours a day, the pay eighty-five cents to a dollar and a quarter. There were numerous accidents. Men were sometimes ripped in two before the saws could be stopped.

There were many Germans and Irish in the mills. On Saturday pay night no good women stirred out of the house without a strong man at her side. Two constables were required to keep the drunks on Main Street from falling under the buggy wheels. In the six blocks between the levee and the Randall House at the

corner of Sixth Street there were fifty-eight saloons. Iowa's prohibition law came early, but to Winslow, as to other river towns,
it made no difference. The proprietors of the saloons were
brought into court once a month to pay a fine of ten dollars and
costs, the equivalent of a license fee.

But it took a rafting crew to make the town really lively. While
in the early days the raftsmen were all from the Northwest, later,
boys from Winslow took to the river. There were Winslow men
on almost every raft. And there were the same bums who came
back to the town each season, starved, ragged, seeking a berth for
a single trip, enough money for a drunk. They were known by
their nicknames, "St. Louis Blackie," "Silver," "The Tomcat."
They had no other names. Fierce Captain Cameron would walk
along the levee and kick one sleeping bundle of rags after another. "You, Walleye, and you, Mugs, go on board the *Fanny
Harris* and report to the mate." Having in common a proud,
willful independence, raftsmen took the town when they turned
it to pleasure.

The floating brothels, rigged on small barges, knew them.
Often these vessels of pleasure would follow a raft, or two or
three rafts, to the mills at Winslow, sure of patronage when the
crew was paid off. The roosters went often to the German beer
garden, the Schutzen park, on the edge of town. Sometimes they
were admitted, sometimes not, depending upon the state of the
Schutzen Verein's treasury. But always they fought, and each
time the Germans lost and swore never again to traffic with such
brutes. After a particularly violent battle, Heinrich Schenk, lawyer for the Schutzen Verein, had twenty raftsmen haled up before the justice of the peace. The small rooms would just hold the
hulking defendants and two or three constables. The complain-
ing witnesses had to wait outside. At intervals Heinrich would
lean out of the window to call, "Send up another black eye," or,
"Another one with teeth out if you please."

Certain of these roosters acquired awful reputations in Winslow. Big Jack Manville had been a Winslow boy, but no one was
so feared. Once he smashed a dozen windows on Main Street
before the constabulary could control him. He appeared in court

the next day, sober and subdued, a dignified colossus. Two or three merchants had come to make sure that he was at last put in jail, but when they saw Big Jack in the flesh they lost their courage. For a time he waited and then he said, rising with a proud contempt, "If there's not going to be any action around here I'm going home." Home he went.

You could tell when a neighbor had come off the river; his clothes would be decorating the back fence in order that they might be deloused by the sun and air. Men were compelled to shed their river clothes in the barn or woodshed before conscientious wives would allow them to step into the house. Sometimes raftsmen bound downriver to a mill below Winslow would steal an hour or two at home. A ribald story passed around that Shady Ashcraft kept his little boy on the riverbank watching for his return. At the approach of Shady's raft, the youngster, acting upon explicit instructions, ran like hell and bore this warning to his mother, "Go on to bed, ma, because pa's about to step on shore."

Many raftsmen spent the winter at home in pleasant idleness; they danced, played cards, called on the girls, bought a Stetson hat and a pair of box-toed shoes. There were boatyards at Winslow, busy through the winter, employing skilled caulkers and woodworkers who made good wages and spent freely. In the spring there were two or three launchings that called for all the rancid butter from the country round about to grease the ways.

Respectable mothers despaired of their children. Little girls who wore white aprons to school came home in tears; some big girl or loutish boy had pulled their braids. In summer, despite the grim vigilance of the roosters, most boys lived on and along the big rafts that were tied up by the mills, waiting to approach the log chute. It was a magnificent place to swim and dive, but a constant peril; slip under the shifting web of logs and it was ten to one that you would never come up alive.

The roosters were heroes who sometimes accepted the tribute of youthful awe. One afternoon two giants were bathing on the edge of the raft. "C'mere, bub," called the one, "and I'll show you something." On his chest was tattooed a fully rigged ship; dangling over his shoulder and trailing down his spinal column went a very realistic rope that disappeared below the small of his back. He bent over to let the boys read the legend that was tattooed along the rope. It said, "More rope where this came from." The two men roared with laughter.

The sawdust piles had become mountain ranges. Rizen Abbott — called Goat Abbott for some obscure, long-lost reason — was already a rich man. On Abbott's Slough he had three great mills topped by three tall stacks, and the square piles of sweet-smelling lumber covered acres of ground in his yards. He was a broad, thick man with a great generous slash of a mouth. When the sleighing was good, he often gathered all the children of the neighborhood into his big sleigh, took them for a swift ride, and then bought them boots with red tops and copper toes and a box of candy all around. But each day at six o'clock he was stationary; he would take more whiskey, but it would not stay down. He was full of whiskey; he carried in four or five pockets half-pint flasks that contained what was for him a single drink. And yet his vigorous mind seemed always clear and sharp. Mrs. Abbott, who was a proud woman, had few friends and even they said that she was distant, cold. She wanted their one son, Will, to be a gentleman, to go to Harvard College and be a gentleman. Goat Abbott wanted his son in the lumber business.

Abbott, Westbrook and the Devines were all in the combine that old man Weyerhaeuser had formed. J. L. Westbrook was a hard, God-fearing man; he wore a little fringe of whiskers, like a half-moon around his face. The stern tenets of his Methodism would not permit him to work his men on Sundays. On Saturday at midnight it was his custom to order his steamboats, which were to return north for rafts, restocked with provisions. The Westbrook foreman would turn over to the grocer a long, long list of supplies, and the grocer and his wife and two younger brothers would toil until midnight Sunday to fill the orders and get the supplies aboard. Plainly Westbrook did not hold himself responsible for the souls of the grocer and his family. It was in this custom that the hatred between the grocer's family, the Sewells, and the Westbrooks originated; it is the most distinguished hatred in Winslow, having come down intact to the present day.

Once when J. L.'s younger son, Philomen, was eighteen, J. L. became enraged at something the boy said, and there in the street he thrashed him with an axe handle until he broke the boy's arm. It was late at night and only a few onlookers gathered. When J. L. strode away, they picked up Philomen, carried him into a saloon and went for a doctor. In this way, the town says, the old man broke Philomen's spirit. But J. L. had an older son, Horatio, who was as mean as his father.

The Devines were easier, pleasanter. They were French-Irish and they liked to live in easy, pleasant style. Old man Devine came to Winslow with one silver dollar in his pocket. But as soon as he began to make money he let his family spend it. They built a house on Fifth Avenue, young Bernadotte and Paris went away to a military school, and Antoinette, Louisa, and Fanny were sent to Ferry Hall in Lake Forest.

There were others whose fortunes were mounting as the logs flowed in a ceaseless brown tide down the broad river. There were the Tollivers and the Bradleys and the Gardiners. But Goat Abbott, Westbrook, and the Devines ruled the roost. Sometimes their mills and their lumber piles burned — burned for days — and all the town was black and reeked with smoke. The women made sandwiches and coffee for the fire fighters. The men built the mills up again and scorned the insurance, which cautious underwriters held at fabulous rates.

These three families were making money in undreamed-of sums. They were not the biggest on the upper river, they were under the domination of Weyerhaeuser. But they had long since become the richest men in Winslow, outstripping pompous Peter Van Hewitt Smith, who came West with six hundred thousand dollars and a number of grandiose ideas, which he swiftly and painfully relinquished. The pace on the river had become faster, harder. During the rafting season Abbott and the others lived on their boats between Winslow and Beef Slough. For three weeks, during the big fight over the Beef Slough boom, Goat never took off his clothes. The rafting crews worked fourteen, eighteen, twenty hours a day. For one entire week the river before Winslow was covered with logs for seven miles, and people came from around the whole country on a Sunday in mid June to see the spectacle.

Goat Abbott, wearied at last of his wife's nagging, built a huge house — all turrets and towers and porches and three upstairs balconies and a stained-glass window on the stairway, twenty feet high. Goat had them panel one room in white pine with a low polish. He said he liked the smell of the wood, and after all, it was the way he'd made his money, wasn't it?

A little later Louisa Devine married Philomen Westbrook. The two families built them a handsome house on the bluff in back of the town. From the wide windows of their drawing room (Louisa, who had lived in New York, said it was not a parlor) you could look out over the hills and the flat roofs of the town to the shining river. There were separate quarters for the servants over the stables. No one had ever called them servants before, to say nothing of having special quarters for them. Later on, old man Devine built another big house on the bluff for Antoinette and Billy Rickard and another one for himself, so that the three houses dominated all of Winslow.

The Devines, said the town, with an emotion that was somewhere between envy and admiration, were living high, wide, and handsome. It was Bernadotte Devine who built the first houseboat. He called it the *Princess* for his sister Fanny. That had been Fanny's name when she was a child with long, carefully curled golden hair — The Little Princess. And to the towboat that pushed the *Princess,* Bernadotte gave the name the *Duchess.* That first houseboat introduced a grand, lazy, blissful sort of life. The logging business was almost at an end. They were all rich, they could take time, or at any rate, the Devines could.

The *Princess* was fitted out by decorators from Marshall Fields: eight bedrooms, five baths, a main saloon, a dining saloon, the master's library, and a verandah deck that ran the whole length of the boat, bright with blooming plants along the rail and hanging baskets of fern. There were no cares, no concerns, no smoke, no vibration—floating dreamily along on the *Princess,* one was even hardly aware of the puffing *Duchess.* It was a great life, a timeless, dreamlike existence.

The best of the Devine crews were always assigned to the *Duchess.* And the black stewards on the *Princess* were chosen for their musical ability as much as for anything else. Toward the late afternoon the *Princess* and the *Duchess* would head into some quiet slough and the whole party would go swimming along a sandbar, then picnic there, and in the moonlight listen to the blacks singing on the deck and strumming their banjos. On the verandah deck were hammocks that held two, a hammock for each couple, and the official chaperone was not too watchful.

The Devines had friends all up and down the river, and before each trip hampers of the finest champagne and claret and liqueurs and whiskies were carried on board. Stop at Burlington and have a party; it was there that the new Brussels carpet in the main saloon was initiated with spilled champagne (that was the trip on which they visited the distillery towns, from Peoria to Louisville, up the Ohio). Nothing to do, nothing in the wide world to do, through long, lazy afternoons; the green, mysterious shore slipping timelessly past the rail.

Soon there were other houseboats. The Tollivers built and equipped the *Summer Girl* and the *Chaperone,* and old Westbrook was pried loose from the cash for the *Eva* and the *Uncle Tom.* But the Devines managed to lead. They started the Outing Club. Paris advanced the money to build the big, gabled clubhouse on a point of land at Weehasket, five miles below Winslow, where the river sweeps by in all its swelling might and majesty. The *Winslow Gazette* said, and with justice, that no verandah in the Middle West could boast a finer view. There were twenty suites, each with a bedroom, bath and small sitting room; card rooms; three dining rooms. The ladies spent long, carefree weeks there; husbands drove down in the afternoon in smart turnouts with a groom up behind. Visitors from Minneapolis and Chicago liked to stop at the Outing Club.

How they overshadowed the town, the Devines and the Westbrooks. Goat Abbott was away most of the time; he had

branched out into railroads and timber on the West Coast, with
his son Will, who had gone to Harvard and was a gentleman, but
good at business, too. Mrs. Abbott was shut away entirely; she
lived with an old servant in the big house and now and then you
saw her sallow, withered face at the window. She refused to meet
her oldest friends; they said it was because she was so unhappy
with Goat. So the Devines and the Westbrooks ruled the town
alone. They were like the reigning families of some middle-Euro-
pean principality.

Each detail of their life was the subject of discussion. When
Paris Devine was drowned off the *Princess,* three thousand people packed the levee to see them bring his body ashore. The town
knew very well that Antoinette was not getting along with Billy
Rickard; the report of a separation hovered in the air for years.
The very appearance of their children, riding in a high-wheeled
wicker pony cart with a watchful British-looking governess, was
enough to set every curtain along the street to fluttering. Other
children stopped their play to stare with awe that was not unmixed with envy at the sight of the sleek Shetland pony and the
smart little cart and the youngster who held the reins with such
casual assurance. On their second trip to London, Louisa and
Philo bought a Daimler and brought it back to Winslow; it was
the first car the town had seen nearby. Billy Rickard drank too
much and ran with women, that was established. Louisa and
Philo and their children traveled between California, New York,
and Europe, with brief stopovers at the big house on the bluff
above the town. Old man Westbrook was dying of cancer, but he
got scant sympathy from the town; everyone knew that Horatio
would get the money and conserve it as meanly as his father had.

All the mills were closed now except one that Goat Abbott
kept open to saw the few logs that still came down from the
north. The sawdust mountains were brown and discolored; they
had begun to settle into the river. There were great mines of rotting lath and waste lumber where the yards had been. The tempo
of the town was slower. A number of the best pilots left for the
Yukon; a few found berths in the government service; others settled down to loaf away their lives or take to modest farming.

Iowa was dry in earnest, but Fairview, across the Mississippi in Illinois, was dripping wet, and a stream of thirsty Iowans poured through Winslow and over the high bridge. Returning very drunk, they gave to Main Street a faint semblance of the wild and bloody past. The high bridge had never paid before; it now became as the mines of Ophir — liquor was smuggled across in wheelbarrows, baby buggies, pushcarts, anything on wheels.

The old-timers were falling away. Jumbo Bradley committed suicide. Goat Abbott had a stroke in Seattle, but not before he had made sure of a proper entry into heaven. "They may be right; you can't tell," he was often heard to say as age crept upon him. "These Christians, these church folks, may be right. Anyhow I can't afford to take a chance like that." He gave to the Episcopal church handsome carved choir stalls of white pine, an altar, a communion service of handwrought gold, a new organ, a new roof, and an endowment. He left an estate of $17 million and when his son Will died six years later it had appreciated to $33 million. Mrs. Abbott lives on, more withered and yellow, seldom venturing from the house, never from the big yard and the protection of the high cedar hedges around it. Intruders are turned away by Anna, who has been with the Abbotts for thirty-eight years. The Westbrook fortune went, when the old man died after incredible months of torture, to Horatio, who was to administer it for Philo; the two sisters, Ella and Jennie; and himself.

The high life came to an end with the swift unreality of melodrama. Closed away in his massive fortresslike house on the little park off Fifth Avenue, Horatio occupied himself entirely with preserving the great fortune — forty million was the rumor — he had inherited from his father, administering the income to the others of the family with all the niggardliness the law would allow, dominating the town with the cold threat of his personality. The Devines, upon the death of the head of the family, ventured into southern pine and high finance. Within a few years they took such severe losses that their way of living had to be drastically curtailed. Louisa and Philo and the children came back for a month or two in the summer, but the rest of the year they were at Pasadena. Antoinette divorced Rickard, supporting

him in a sanitarium for alcoholics until his death. Fanny termi-
nated a romance long frustrated and married Captain Henry
Robaire of her father's fleet; he had one quarter Chippewa Indian blood. As Mrs. Robaire she developed a giddy streak and
was given to becoming tipsy, a foolish smile on her foolish face
beneath the absurd crown of graying yellow curls.

Although an air of quiescence and decay hangs over Winslow,
its character persists, stubborn and unregenerate. Many of the
figures of the gaudy past live on, like figures from some heroic
frieze buried under wind-blown sand and lost to time, difficult
and incomprehensible. Big Jack Manville, Captain Cameron,
Mr. Jabez, and many more survive. They are not unlike certain
houses that have been covered by a pretentious generation with
thin coatings of stucco, a meager surface that does not conceal
their sharp, uncompromising angularity. Big Jack lives alone in a
small yellow cottage; from his front door he can see the river; his
mate's license hangs over the radio. Mr. Jabez sits on the rotting
remains of a sheer boom and talks of the past in his fine Irish
speech. Captain Cameron is eighty-six but he looks as though he
had been carved out of hickory, as tough and as limber, with the
fringe of stiff-looking whiskers still encircling his face.

Winslow bears a resemblance to the dying New England
coastal towns of a generation ago. There are many spinsters, odd
crustacea cast upon the beach by the receding wave of energy.
Some of them are so old that they can remember as little girls
being brought to the West by their fathers, from Boston and
Gloucester and New Bedford. The river attracted these New
Englanders. Winslow was destined to be a great town, one to
rival Chicago. Wilda Cranch's father came west to start an insurance company in Winslow. It failed swiftly, and Mr. Cranch died
of the galloping consumption. That happened in 1857; Wilda
was four years old; but when she speaks of it today there is the
shadow of forgotten emotion in the shriveled parchment of her
face.

The Monday girls must be seventy — yes, seventy-five — but
to Winslow they are still the Monday girls. Olive Read lives
alone in the big, shuttered house at the end of Chestnut Street;

children play in the tangled undergrowth and shrubbery of the lawn until she comes out to drive them off; neighbors leave custards and small loaves of new-baked bread on her doorstep. Effie Law was with her father, the captain, when he was killed in the explosion of the *Silver Wave* near New Orleans. Since that time she has lived on the charity of the town, repaying generosity with mild humors of her imbecility. Until a recent date, a whole tribe of idiots lived and bred in a cluster of squalid huts along the riverbank, beside the deserted button factory. One family's reputed ignorance of the taboos pertaining to incest was the source of three or four of the more furtive jokes in the town — the kind told in a shocked whisper at the Winslow Ladies' Literary Society and to the accompaniment of guffaws of laughter in Frankie Jonas's pool hall.

The young had begun to go away. Winslow held so little for them. Ambition drew them to Chicago, to the coasts, east and west. They complained that Winslow was dead. But returning for a brief vacation to see family and the few friends who remained, they found the town changing beyond recognition. Thanks to river transportation, the beginning of the barges, and the crisscross of railroads, a half dozen eastern companies had established branches bringing in executives and administrators, and offering jobs that created a settled prosperity.

These newcomers knew little and cared less about the past. They were part of a new Winslow that is only by coincidence on the river. The stamp of the old is rapidly disappearing. Even those industries that grew out of the lumber boom are passing. They are dismantling the sash-and-door factory and selling it for junk. Here an old house has fallen into ruin. Georgia Devine, a third generation and distant connection of the family, stopping off for a week between Santa Barbara and New York, complained that at the country club she had hardly known anyone. They were those new people, new faces. She left after four days.

The Little Princess died the other day, and this was an opportunity for the righteous to write a very moral epitaph to the whole long, crowded period of history. Fanny was found drowned in her bath, whether accidentally or not will never be known. Captain Robaire had departed three weeks before with the contents of their joint safety deposit box. It had not contained much, the town said, but at least it would have given Fanny a decent burial. As it was, Horatio Westbrook and four others put in a hundred dollars each for a modest funeral. Fanny had quarreled long before her death with those members of her own family who had retained any part of the original Devine fortune. Louisa was telegraphed to, but her address was uncertain and no answer came. Antoinette Rickard, living obscure and forgotten in the south of France, cabled an appeal to Horatio. That was all.

Because so much has gone on there, the town is full of tales. Every old-timer who walks down the street has a history that the rest of the town can furnish on demand. They live more and more in the past, feeding upon reminiscences of the great days. There are times when Mr. Jabez dwells completely in a world that has long since disappeared, speaking of friends long dead as though they might come round the corner to question his story, and referring to landmarks obliterated years ago as though they stood shining and new to the gaze of the smallest child. Beneath the present, the new Winslow, lives the memory of this past.

14

The Lost River

The River that I knew was a remote, lost river. It was as far from the industrial world of the 1900s as the upper reaches of the Amazon, and as seldom visited, as lonely, as quiet. The forests were gone; the packets were gone. With them went all the noisy, shouting, pushing mob, leaving a curious interlude of peace, of solitude, of weariness perhaps. It was as special, as rare, in many ways as any of the lusty periods that had gone before.

The river in front of Allenton was wide and clear. Beneath the spidery ramp of the high bridge was the dock — the boatyard if it could be called that — where ten to twenty boats were moored, pleasure launches for the most part, with here and there a fisherman's flatboat or a clammer's scow hung with odd-shaped clamming hooks. Usually here at the foot of Fourth Street you would find someone tinkering at a boat; that was part of the pleasure of ownership.

Because my father was not a river man, not adept in the skills of the river acquired through years of familiarity and experience, we never owned a launch. But each summer we went up the river with the Jamiesons to stay for a time at their cabin at Deer River. That voyage held all secret strangeness, all lost solitude. It was not a casual excursion embarked upon with rash impetuousness, but an expedition planned with unusual care and forethought. The burden fell upon the Jamiesons and for the most part upon Captain Jamieson. Our chief responsibility was to present ourselves at the foot of Fourth Street with our luggage, fishing tackle, and certain generous hampers of food which our household had prepared.

Captain Jamieson was in command from the moment that the party assembled at the small floating dock. He was commodore, engineer, and purser all in one. We regarded him, my brother and I, in every particular a river man. He was tall and straight and lean as an arrow, with a mane of silver white hair above his lean, sunburned face. He spoke with the river drawl and moved with a slow, deliberate tempo — except at the moment of departure, when he displayed a sudden and surprising speed, casting off line, turning over the engine, giving orders to his wife at the wheel.

Captain Jamieson's launch was the *Josie,* named for his wife. Although he had commanded many a fine steamboat, the *Josie* satisfied him, he took pride in her. And indeed she was a boat to try the skill and patience of the most resourceful commander. The main difficulty was in her engine, which was of one cylinder, and that about the size of a coffeepot. When we first cast off from the dock, there was almost always a crisis when the engine of the *Josie* died and Captain Jamieson spun the cantankerous flywheel again and again, muttering under his breath and occasionally shouting directions at his wife, "Hold her upstream, Josie, hold over on her there." Sputter, sputter, sputter, went the engine. And all the while we drifted with the swift current under the bridge.

But this crisis was resolved at the moment when Captain Jamieson's patience was absolutely at the boiling point, with the pop-pop-popping of the *Josie*'s motor. We would have the wide, wide river to ourselves. It was marvelous, wonderful. If the engine of the *Josie* was difficult to start, it had the quality, once we were under way, of a fine and stubborn loyalty. Small though it was, it shook the *Josie* with a gentle, regular vibration, carrying us upstream against the current at a rate that must have been, possibly, two to three miles an hour. Objects on the bank had a curious and fascinating fixity. And yet we passed them, inch by inch. The ruined lime kiln, gaunt above the bluff. The ruined lumber mills beneath their great cold chimneys. And the town

itself, that moment when last you saw the spire of the Congrega-
tional church, when the trestle of the high bridge, nothing but a
thread really, disappeared from view.

The women and children were confined to the stern of the
Josie, where there were cushioned seats. Captain Jamieson had
the wheel, and it was my father's privilege to sit beside him in the
bow. But even in that vantage place my father was plainly a
landsman, lacking the nautical air that went with the officer's cap
that Captain Jamieson wore so well, and with none of the fine
quizzicalness with which Captain Jamieson studied the land and
the water, charting our course up the lonely river. There were
marks that we remembered from year to year. One was an anchored buoy that was forever plunging and twisting and leaping
in the racing current of a minor shoal.

A colony of cabins at Swift Water was about half way. Here
the bank of the river was sharply sculptured and the channel
very still and deep and fast. In a grove of great trees the small
cabins stood, and at our hail usually someone would come into
sight. The progress of the *Josie* was so slow, particularly slow
against the sweep of the current at Swift Water, that a long conversation would go on between the boat and the bank. How's the
fishing over in Little Turkey? Oh, pretty good, caught four or five
nice bass over there this morning. River been rising any? Oh,
'bout half a foot, with that rain they had up above. You folks
bound for Deer River, I suppose? And so on, the voices blurred a
little with the popping of the *Josie*'s motor.

There was always a time when my brother and I became rest-
less, the green wall of willows that was the shore holding no sign
of any kind of life to break the drowsy summer afternoon monotony. It was then that Captain Jamieson allowed us, each in his
proper turn, to come forward, past the hot chugging heart of the
Josie, a precarious passage with voices raised in anxious warning.
Seated in the bow, we were permitted — it was a clear stretch of
river — to take the wheel while Captain Jamieson instructed us
in steering. From the response to a turn of a notch or two —
scarcely perceptible to a less eager eye — we derived a grand
sense of nautical power.

The last phase of the voyage was the most perilous. Captain Jamieson had to pilot the *Josie* through Hole-in-the-Wall, a narrow inlet between two islands that gave off from the river into Deer River Slough. At the entrance to Hole-in-the-Wall Captain Jamieson took soundings with a long pole. The engine of the *Josie* was reduced to its lower speed — there were two — and we crept in between the islands, the sweet-smelling willows on either side so close they brushed the top of the boat, the hull scrunching on the sand if it were low water.

There before us was Deer River, a long, wide slough walled off by islands; at the north, screened by trees, was the mouth of Deer River itself; and half obscured in the bright foliage of the low shore were the cabins, odd shaped houses of weathered gray or some bright new color standing awkward and a little apologetic upon high stilts. The sound of the *Josie* never failed to draw some of the summer colony at Deer River down to the bank. We landed — Captain Jamieson, expert with the gangplank, giving a command to Mrs. Jamieson or my father — to be received with a welcome befitting travelers who had concluded such a voyage.

It was a pleasant, carefree life at Deer River. Children had as easy access to water and boats as the children of a South Sea island tribe. Each cabin had two or three scull boats moored in front, and these any child over the age of six might use. The scull boat is a safe boat but nevertheless trim of line and easy to handle. To go exploring alone was the most satisfying thing that one could do; in the mysterious peace the rhythm of the dip of the oars was the only sound. A few hundred yards in any direction and one was out of sight and hearing of the colony, and only a sense of time and the deepening shadows of the shore could draw the explorer back.

Deer River was a microcosm of the town. Mr. Willard, a big, handsome, jovial man who made an excellent income as a salesman of lumber, had one of the finest cabins, to which room after room had been added as though by some process of natural growth. Will Ames, who was said to have become a famous illustrator in the East, had painted pictures on the walls of Mr. Willard's cabin: Hole-in-the-Wall, Swift Water, Big and Little

Turkey — fine, gay-colored murals. Next door was Dr. Houghton's cabin, and next door to Dr. Houghton was Mr. Moriarty, who had been a raftsman in his youth. Farther on lived the Thomassons; he was cashier in the bank. For the most part they were all of the same class, the same group of friends in the town, and through long, lazy afternoons they played bridge whist on the screened verandah of one cabin or another.

Or they fished. Fishing was the only serious occupation at Deer River. In the late afternoon several of the young, with an elder or two to supervise, went seining for minnows off a nearby sandbar. It was in itself a great privilege to walk, holding one end of the net, through the clear, cool water, waist-deep, seeing the silver glint of the school of minnows harried and driven on before. Or armed with this bait, with reels and poles and tackle boxes and hampers of lunch, an early start was made in the morning. Sometimes the men went off alone; sometimes there were family parties.

We would depart in the *Josie,* with two scull boats fastened behind, and go up into Long Tom Slough, which gave onto Christmas Lake. There were an infinite number of such sloughs where for the whole day one would be alone, the only intruders upon a solitude that seemed hitherto never to have been broken. The two ladies and my brother, who was younger, went in one scull boat, and I went with the men. We fished snags for bass and crappies and even, when luck was bad, for sunfish. Meeting at noon to share our lunch, we compared strings and it was humiliating to me if the ladies' boat had been more successful than ours. A three-pound black bass — and they could put up a splendid fight at that size — was enough to make the day a triumph. It was a trophy to display to the assembled colony when we were back at Deer River.

Above all I remember Captain Jamieson's patience. I remember sitting in the stern of a scull boat with my brother, rowing up along Marvel's Island; the errand, if any, is long, long since forgotten. Captain Jamieson rowed with perfect ease. Without seeming effort we glided through the water, our progress marked by the rhythm of the oarlocks, the crisp, clean dip of the oars.

And he talked — about how the river had been in an earlier day, where Indian Head had been before the big flood, and how Hole-in-the-Wall had cut its way through Old and New Catawba; about hunting snipe down on the 'Dosia and where he had had his blind in the duck season last fall. The rhythm of his drawling voice was one with the rhythm of the oars. We were so close to the shore that the smell of the willows was strong and heady, one with the nascent smell of the water itself. In the blue air high above a heron flew on lazy wings. I knew all this with a deep, inner satisfaction; it was the magic of the river that I felt deep down in my bones.

The night cast a spell, too, a spell that one never knew in town. There was a quality of stillness accentuated by mysterious sounds that came from over the dark water — the splash of a fish, a far-off voice. From the verandah of the Jamieson cabin there was barely visible, through Hole-in-the-Wall, a government channel light burning very small and faint, like a minor star against the horizon. And behind you as you stood staring out into the night were the friendly reassuring voices that came from the cabin, the window that was a mellow square of lamplight.

Settling down to sleep you might hear the voices of the elders in the room beyond. And in the faint light from the door you could see on the wall the gun rack, a box of shotgun shells, an old hunting cap with earflaps that were tied over the top — things that told of another life, a sterner, masculine life, which went on at the cabin in the fall. You wondered how it would be to be part of that life, you knew you would be a part of it someday. You were aware of the mysterious all-pervading quiet and then you were asleep.

The far-off, almost dreamlike life of Deer River was in many ways characteristic of the river of the 1900s. Every town on the upper Mississippi had its Deer River, usually more than one summer colony. I never saw a packet in the regular packet service, I never saw a log raft. And yet I think this lost river had its influence on me and my contemporaries, as much perhaps as on the earlier generations who knew it as a turbulent highway for the trade and travel of a continent.

If we had no packets, at least we had excursion boats, which were gaudier, more gilded, more lavishly ornamented with scroll saw work. All-day and afternoon excursions sponsored by church guilds and aid societies were respectable outings, family occasions in which large picnic baskets of the most delectable food played an important part. At night, under a lush August moon, the darkened upper deck was a field of asphodel for lovers who lay in tumbled posture oblivious to passersby, hearing, or not hearing, the faint strains of the orchestra on the deck below. There might be liquor and a fight between young mill hands on a night excursion.

But the finest thing about an excursion boat for the young was the calliope. On a hot, still day the music of a calliope penetrated to the farthest bluffs of the town, summoning to the riverbank every boy who could free himself from the toils of duty or parental oversight. Envy gnawed at the sight of the fortunate ones who were marching, not without a certain smug, gloating self-satisfaction, up the gangplank. All the time the boat was loading the calliope kept up its maddening music, beautiful and exciting and yet a taunt. The man who played it was plainly visible, seated before his little keyboard on the upper deck, one of the elect of the earth. As the boat prepared to back out into the stream and the last belated excursionist scurried over the gangplank, the calliope player broke into some rousing tune such as a "Hot Time in the Old Town Tonight." And as the boat, in all its pride and prowess, steamed out into the channel, a last flare of music came back to the crowd left behind on the bank. Returning at supper time, or late at night, the calliope struck up again to remind the town of what pleasures the river afforded.

There was a winter magic, too, days when the light came from the sky with a cold shining quality. As far as one could see there was the hard blue sheen of the frozen river. It was so still, only an occasional rumbling and cracking of the ice, as though the fierce current struggled somewhere far below to free itself from the armor of winter. And it seemed that one might look through the crystalline ice far down into the dark heart of the stream.

Skating, you went often beyond the bounds prescribed in repeated warnings. You went into the remote frozen fastness of Cattail Slough. It was like Siberia; it had that quality of being at the end of the world, which heightened as the sun began to go down. In the odd lingering dusk, the ice itself seemed to glow with a frozen fire borrowed from the sun, now quite lost behind the bluffs. You skated home from this Arctic outpost, cold, so cold, and very weary, but sustained by the glory of one who has seen far places and mysterious horizons.

At night there were flares, voices shouting, young couples skating in long processions two by two. It was exciting and dangerous. There were air holes to be leaped across, gorges where the thick ice piled up in jagged sheets. The stars were infinitely cold and clear and far off against the night sky. It was another river in winter, but no less magical.

The Mississippi had for my generation no connotation of utility. In the deep South a few boats persisted in the cotton trade. Their owners, usually the captain himself, made an often precarious living from the business that the railroads had left. They called at isolated plantations and landing stages not on the railroad. Certain of these boats could accommodate passengers and they tried to maintain, successfully in several instances, the high standards of food and service set by the packets immediately after the Civil War. A kind of loyalty grew up between planter and captain, a personal intimacy that assured the planter's business to the steamboat year after year. And in return the captain did innumerable favors, quite beyond the province of an impersonal railroad, for the planter. Showboats, and even a few trading scows, thrived in distant bayous and the farther reaches of tributary streams.

But this was rare and exceptional. There was a boat or two on the Arkansas, a boat or two on the Red River, an occasional boat on the Mississippi below Greenville, a fleet of coal barges on the Ohio, and there were always government boats in one service or another. But otherwise the wide river was swept bare. One might travel an entire day without seeing another boat, unless it were a government dredge or a little launch. One form of travel and transportation had entirely supplanted the other. Even on the railroads the movement from north to south existed in a relatively minor way, as a tributary of the east and west stream. The river would accumulate more and more a quaint antiquarian interest. Adventurers in canoes made expeditions down it, latter day La Salles rediscovering the great river with the zeal of first comers. These intrepid voyagers invariably wrote their memoirs, creating a curious literature of rediscovery that has grown of sufficient size to occupy not a little space in the library of the river.

A steamboat was a curious survival, a picturesque anachronism. It was inevitable, perhaps, that the life that had once flourished on the Mississippi system should be romanticized, sentimentalized, out of all semblance to what it had actually been. It became a part of the quavering moonlight-and-magnolias tradition of the deep South. Moldering Natchez, decaying New Orleans were adorned with this spurious "culture" of the early river — blacks caroling dressed-up folk songs from the prow of Currier and Ives steamboats, prettified legends of romantic showboats. Beneath this disguise the unchanging river flowed to the sea.

15

Down Government River

From the deck of the *Mark Twain,* loading a cargo at the wharf, the skyscrapers of Saint Paul rise out of the dusk like cliffs; and towering behind them are mountainous cloud banks. The lights go on, and this great backdrop glows in the darkness. The *Mark Twain* is a new boat, brand shining new, from the big black and nickeled stove in her galley to the beautiful diesel motors in her hold. Her barges are being loaded with pig iron for this first voyage of 1934. Crotchety officials must inspect her with proprietary airs that somehow seem doubly incongruous and false because they belong so completely to landsmen.

As a privileged passenger, a guest, I am bound down the river system that the government is remaking from north to south for several thousand miles. This is the new order ordained by planners and engineers in Washington with their outposts scattered all along the course of the unruly stream they were plotting to tame. Given the wild unreconstructed past, it would seem impossible. Yet they are confident they are on the way, these plotters drawing on the treasury of the United States year after year.

Long before dawn we pull away from the wharf and the cliff that is Saint Paul. The trees are just beginning to show green on the distant banks. It is the opening of the season of navigation, and we alone are on the river to inaugurate it. All day long it is so, and in the big generous pilothouse we seem emissaries sent out from another world to the lonely wilderness. The humming of the wireless in the shining white wireless room is our only contact with that other world.

We in the pilothouse have a sense of pleasant isolation. Jim Graves is an old-time pilot, given to fine flourishes, polishing off a difficult crossing with a certain artistry that is pure art for art's sake. He is very straight and tall with a fine profile and iron gray hair. Snubbed on to the stubby prow of the *Mark Twain* are twelve barges, three abreast, a stiff unwieldy tow that is more than twice as long as the *Mark Twain* itself. A shred of red cloth flaps from a flagpole — it is really only a tall willow withe — on the middle barge of the front rank. Captain Reed bends low, shading his eyes with his hand to line up this flag with a government diamond board that is only a white spot against the distant bluff.

The other pilot is Nils Pedersen, a quiet young Norwegian who carries in his mind the outline of innumerable fjords along his native coast. Perhaps that is why he learned the river so easily and why he is regarded as so fine a pilot. It is a curious team, the old man and the young man, the old river and the new.

Lake Pepin is full of floating ice, rotten ice, Pilot Graves says it is. The iron hull of the *Mark Twain* breasts a way through it with a faint tinkling sound. One can understand how boats were lost in Lake Pepin. The distant shore seems very small even in the bright sharp sunlight. And when storms lash this lake, which is really only a wide place — but a very wide place — in the Mississippi, the shore can look much farther off.

Against the low dark bluff on the Wisconsin side is a little town, yellow and white squares that look very small and clean and somehow lonely, like the river itself. It is the village of Alma. The high palisades of the river tower above us, gaunt and beautiful. There is the mouth of the Chippewa, and on the opposite shore the site of a logging town, a wild, roaring boom town of the lumber era. It is all gone and even the scars that it must have left are covered over by the rank growth of willows. It is a joy to watch Nils Pedersen run the railroad bridge at Winona, so easily and surely.

Against the shore is a line of quarterboats, half a dozen or more, where the men live who are working on the dredging operations two or three miles below. A cook in a white apron and hat stands at the rail with his assistants to watch us pass. They wave idly. The long suction pipe of the dredger extends from the shore out almost into the channel.

At nightfall you sometimes see the light tenders making their lonely rounds. Evening is the finest time in the pilothouse. Then all the skill of the pilot is called forth and we, the audience, sit in silent admiration. There is a beautiful stillness, a peaceful quiet that comes down. Even the pounding of the engines is far off, somehow unrelated to the gentle vibration that rattles the pilothouse windows. The bridge at La Crosse is strung with a thousand lights, like a new constellation hung up in the night sky. The town itself gives off a soft glow. Jim Graves slips on the switch and our searchlights, long trembling beams of bluish light, pick up here the massive stone pier of the bridge, there a corner of the wharf, and a man, very small in the intense white arc.

Morning and we are at Dubuque, a gray mist rising from the cool river. Though is is Sunday, the terminal is open and the roustabouts are ready. Nils controls the big new boat with an easy touch of the hand, jockeying the loaded and unloaded barges from one open doorway to another, like freight cars before a warehouse on the edge of a shipping yard. The tow is light. Because it is early in the season, says Captain Reed. Like river captains from time immemorial he seems a secondary figure in the presence of his pilots. And yet he is the master, well aware of the working of the system of which he is a part. Every hour Captain Reed gets a report from the wireless room of the position of each boat on the upper Mississippi division.

Sunday dinner is a harvest hands' meal — chicken and everything that goes with it. There is another fleet of quarterboats, under the tow this time of a substantial-looking steamboat, the *Bessie Able*. It is such an unusual sight that we line up at the rail and salute each other. Two fleets of the government's inland navy passing in the big stream. It is curious to think back to the tax sources of this peaceable navy and the ultimate provider, the consumer, who must pay the bill. It is a sight, these two government fleets at hail.

And then the river is empty again, the bluffs like great ragged walls slowly crumbling into ruin. At Clinton there are three bridges to run, but it is simpler now that the government has put years of work into the river. This is beautiful country, with landmarks of the old days. The little town of Le Claire, like a New England town lost in the hills, was once an important boat-building center, and under the wine-glass elm that still stands on the levee, roosters from the rafts slept off their drink.

We go through the locks at Rock Island; it is a complicated process getting the tow into line for this narrow passage. There is enormous activity on the new dam, great bulwarks of masonry, dredgers, construction railways, giant cranes, and men moving everywhere like pigmies over this massive molehill that the army is throwing up in the river. How the old boys would stare if they could see it, the old boys who braved the rapids in jigsaw tinder-boxes.

It is greener now, the young shimmering green of the willows. Another night and another misted dawn and we are well below Lake Keokuk, getting on to Saint Louis. Hannibal has a fine new highway bridge. The town has grown away from the levee and looks remote and respectable, like any other mid-western main street. On the eastern shore the bluffs are far off or they have disappeared altogether. This begins to look like the lower river.

Saint Louis is a vague black cloud in the distance. The filthy Missouri comes rushing in with its burden of silt from distant plains. The great refineries at Wood River, the mills at Alton and Granite City, spill tons of refuse into the stream. Great oil smears float, black and iridescent, on the surface. Fish that you catch below the refineries are not fit to eat, says Nils. The river is a sewer, ugly and brown and burdened with the offal of cities.

The industrial jungle thrusts up against the sky on either bank, black and uncompromising. On the Illinois shore are the packing plants of Armour, the aluminum company of Mellon, the steel corporation that was absorbed by Pittsburgh. East Saint Louis is incredibly hideous, like some imagined hell. This is the result of the absenteeism that Micajah Tarver foresaw nearly a century ago. But Saint Louis has somehow, perhaps by the very stubbornness of its great sprawling bulk, preserved something of its old character.

The passenger, who is a passenger only by special permit, must change boats here to the *Herbert Hoover* — oh, ironic name — for the trip down the lower river. The Saint Louis terminal has all the efficiency of a modern port, with marvelous loading devices and freight elevators. Leaving in the morning we pass under Captain Eads's bridge, fragile and light, in sharp contrast to the heavy mass that is Saint Louis. The stretch of river from here to Cairo is one that requires constant effort. In the first five hours we pass at least five different dredging outfits, with dredger, quarterboats, all complete. And there is a constant succession of "hurdles," wings of crushed stone and willow branches built out into the stream.

Captain Shannon of the *Herbert Hoover* has seen more than sixty years of service on the Mississippi and yet he seems still tough and strong. He explains how the hurdles create land through the accumulation of silt. It is a very rapid process, so rapid that in ten years land of wonderful fertility is made. That land belongs to the owner of the riparian rights and Captain Shannon remarks, with a sly understanding of the ways of politicians, that this work is usually done for those owners who have a political pull. Two trim little motorboats come speeding up the river and Captain Shannon understands the significance of this phenomenon too. "Lieutenant Standby and Major ComeAlong would both have to have their own boats, couldn't ride together in the same boat." This, then, is the admiralty of the inland navy on an inspection tour.

"Well, we often wonder how so-and-so got his job," says Captain Shannon, wise in the ways of this government river, "can't figure it out for several months; then we learn he's the cousin of congressman somebody-or-other. A man can get a job like that but if he's downright incompetent he has a hard time holding it."

He expresses a grievance common on the river — that the men in the service of the government barge line are not classified under civil service, which would make them secure in tenure and eligible to pensions; but they are subject to federal pay cuts.

We are passing the Sainte Genevieve landing. The church spire of the little lost town, isolated even from the river when the Mississippi made one of its sudden, cantankerous changes, is just visible over the trees. On the Illinois shore the long fertile plain sweeps away to distant hills that are half hidden in the spring haze.

Cairo is the destination of the *Herbert Hoover.* It is after dark as we round into the Ohio and pull alongside the wharf. This is the town that was to have been the Metropolis of the West, a crossroads where commerce would inevitably accumulate. They tell you that the whole town is on the government since the railroad moved its shops away; if not on the river payroll, then on government relief. It is Saturday night and the young are loitering on the street corners, males only, the females, elderly and matronly, are in the drug store. In a car, a party of young, males and females, brandish newly bought pints of whiskey; liquor is displayed in a dozen windows along the brief main street.

In the tradition of the past, Cairo is wide open on Sunday; sallow, pinched-looking men gather at every card table in the chief saloon; and above is the crap game where the chief engineer laments his loss of forty-two dollars. The streets have a desolate Sunday quality, grim rows of gray packing boxes, which may explain the crowded saloons.

Cairo is the home of Pilot Daniels's girl and he likes Cairo. Here, obviously, he is one of the elect of the earth, and at the age of twenty-six. He owes a handsome new car, which he uses during the brief time he has in port. Pilot Daniels has a certain eagerness, a certain shy kind of pride, an obvious liking for his job, and, too, for the salary of $260 a month attached to it. He comes from West Virginia, from a little town eighty miles from the Kanawha River.

I change this time to the *Minnesota,* which embarks with the tow barges that the *Herbert Hoover* brought from Saint Louis. Here is still another kind of pilot, a "child of nature," with an apparently native aptitude for getting the boat and its big unwieldy tow through the river. He comes on board from shore leave in a chocolate brown suit, fawn-colored hat with chocolate brown ribbon, faintly orange-colored tie, and fawn-colored silk shirt, and changes at once into carpet slippers and corduroy pants that gape over his fat belly. He tells a long story of "Paayggy" who runs the whorehouse in Cairo. "Ah put thuhty-one dollahs in uh mechanical piano last night and nevah got hahdly a drink of that whiskey them othah boys bought." On watch just before dusk he talks, in a richly sentimental vein, about getting home to Memphis and his wife and little girl.

Jones, who is the other pilot on the *Minnesota,* is his exact opposite. "One of those finicky Mark Twain pilots," says Captain Andrews with contempt. He comes to a point everywhere, with his long pointed face, pointed shoes, a little belly that seems to come to a point, and shrewd little water-colored eyes. More than ever, he is on his dignity, because on the upward journey he cut in too close to the bank and hit an oil barge of the Standards' fleet. So he is in disgrace and under orders to leave the boat at Memphis and go by train to Saint Louis, where he must give an accounting to the barge line offices for the accident. There is some feeling that he was not to blame, since the barge was anchored too far out in the stream, and that he is being unfairly treated. Captain Andrews has no patience with Jones's wounded dignity. "These old pilots are too damn fussy," he says. "Things have changed. Time was when pilots was so God almighty scarce you was waiting on them all the time. Now we've trained up a lot of young ones. And we can fire 'em just the same as we fire a deckhand."

This is the lower river for certain, the never ending green of the shore, the vast cloud banks that rear above the horizon in the blue sky. There is never a sign of life, only the unbroken tracery of the willows. Fifty, sixty years ago, says Captain Andrews, cotton plantations lined the banks, but this is difficult to believe now. In the morning there is a thick smoky fog with the sun all golden through it. A gray smoky heat comes down close and an idle, listless languor settles over the boat. We make a brief stop at Memphis, picking up three more barges.

We acquire at Memphis, too, a relief pilot on his way back to New Orleans. In Pilot Ferrand's slow, drawling talk the pattern of the river unfolds. His grandfather came down from Canada about 1835 to Arkansas Post; his grandmother was the oldest girl in a large family that came from France, tarried briefly in New Orleans, and then also settled at Arkansas Post, where the two were married. Grandfather worked and made enough money in a few years to buy several thousand acres of land, on which he developed a cotton plantation with a dozen slaves. Pilot Ferrand, as a boy, used to see the steamboats that ran from Memphis up the Arkansas River come to the plantation landing for the family cotton.

Against all tradition and the desire of his family, he became a river pilot. Those were lean years on the Mississippi; he'd find a berth now with a government dredger, now with a commercial barge line. And when there were no more berths, almost no boats left at all, he learned "the deep sea game," became a pilot with Standard Oil — part of the time out of Baton Rouge, part of the time out of New York — in the Tampico trade to South America and Europe. He talks of astronomy, of how the Southern Cross looks, of heavy seas and going aground off Sandy Hook on Christmas Eve, of how champagne cost sixty cents a bottle in the best nightclub in Hamburg during the deflation.

But at the end of five years he came back to the river. It seemed to him that that was where he belonged. He knows every foot of the lower river with a serene, unshakeable knowledge. In his face there is the kind of contentment that seems the reward of a wanderer who has come home. He lives with his wife and child in New Orleans, pronounced "New Orrrrle-e-ens," and says, "You'll nevah find anothah town in these states like New Orrrrle-e-ens."

After a day in which the endless green shore has scarcely been broken, a day of brilliant sun and remote white clouds that give a feeling as though the Gulf were just around the next bend, we come upon Vicksburg. Here the river is very broad and the town high upon the hill stands out sharply against the glowing evening sky. One lumpish skyscraper has a lost, incongruous air. Vicksburg, too, is on the government. Extending along the levee for more than two blocks are dredgers, quarterboats, machine boats — one of the largest fleets we have seen thus far. Under the glare of searchlights at the Vicksburg terminal, our barges are loaded and unloaded, and we prepare to go on.

In the night we pass Natchez upon its austere bluff, and noon brings Huey Long's capital in view. The fantastic old state house is visible from the river, its battlements with their cast-iron crenellations somewhat crumpled, as though they are of papier-mâché left too long in the rain. And beyond, against the horizon, is Huey's new tower, symbol of his power over Louisiana. Captain Andrews supervises one last realignment of the tow. In the small park before the ancient state house are flowering shrubs with great pinkish flowers that burden the warm soft air with their musky smell. And then we are under way again.

Baptiste Lemoyne, the steersman — which means apprentice pilot too — says we will make New Orleans by midnight if things go well. A sense of excitement, of the nearness of the city and the end of the voyage, possesses everyone. The high walls of the levee shut us in. This seems the longest stretch of all, longer even than those interminable days when the green, monotonous shore promised never to end.

But once again city lights flood the night sky. The boys on the lower deck talk of the quarter, with sly references to the cribs, and what brawls they have had there in the past. Now the river becomes like a broad estuary. The rank smell of the sea and shipping labels this a port. Down below they are preparing to dock. Over the edge of the levee, which is one long solid wall of earth, you see the beginning of the city roofs and here and there a far-off light.

It is late, long past midnight. On the prow, steward and cook and cabin boy are waiting, dressed in shore clothes. From somewhere comes close harmony, snatches of a bawdy song. All through the boat there is that excitement of a voyage ending, of a journey done. With two days of shore leave before the *Minnesota* goes north again, anything may happen; that is in the faces of the crew. Here are women and liquor and fine gaming houses. This is New Orleans, the wicked city at the end of the river. It has been so from time immemorial.

16

The Reckoning — 1935

After the sound and fury of the first hundred years of the river's history, and the museumlike era of the lost river, it is possible to take an inventory of what has gone before and what the river has come to. This is one of the concerns Franklin Roosevelt is stressing with his New Deal.

In Washington groups of technicians and analysts began a survey of what remains from the turbulent years that are the subject of this book. It is as though in the midst of still-smouldering ruins they have undertaken to estimate how much has been saved for generations still to be born.

Their reports on the valley at the heart of the continent make plain what has happened in two centuries. In that period — and what is two hundred years? a flick of time, a transient moment — the whole face of the earth has been changed, and changed at a rate such as the world has never known before. All the relationships are not yet understood between the destruction of the forests at the north and the floods that ravage the delta at the south, but it is quite clear that no fragment of leaf mold, no spadeful of sod was disturbed, no beech shoot cut down, without in some measure destroying the balance achieved through aeons of geologic time. What the consequence of that destruction would be, no one for a moment considered; no one thought in those terms. We have only just come to that phase.

There have been floods, it appears, from the beginning. As life along the river took on a more and more settled form, with towns and plantations closely contiguous, the concept of the river began to change. It was no longer a beneficent provision of nature but — in the minds of many who lived under the annual threat of its rises, its freshets, its rages, its whims — the river was an enemy, implacable and relentless. Settled towns and plantations, with their large investments in sugar mills and cotton gins, found it more and more difficult to keep the enemy at bay.

A war with the Mississippi has gone on from the time the first crude dike was thrown up to protect colonial New Orleans. The issue of flood control involved passionate prejudices for which men fought, bled, and died. The various methods of taming and confining floods each attracted their partisans, stubborn and bitter as death itself. Levees, reservoirs, dams — each had its champions, who waged successive campaigns in Congress over how the War Department should shackle the Mississippi. Windy battles they were, filling an infinite number of dusty volumes of the Congressional Record.

From the perspective of the present pause, those debates have a quaint, academic sound. For while the force of the river in flood is a mighty, an awful thing, there was occurring from year to year — unheralded, unknown — a far more catastrophic form of destruction. Man could see the raging torrent of the river; that was an enemy to be dreaded, to flee from. But the erosion of the earth man could neither see with his eyes nor measure with the tools he had created. And yet it continued, ceaselessly, without let or hindrance, from spring freshet through the long, beating rains of the fall.

The concept of the continent of North America, as it lay in the virgin stillness seen by the first settlers, is of a scale of grandeur, an order of beauty, such as we who have invaded it may scarcely perceive. In the valley of the Mississippi a special dispensation of the glacial drift ordained a soil of incredible richness. There grew up a protective cover — grass over the great plains, and forests to the north. The deep soil was honeycombed by the burrowing of insects and plant roots, and made porous by natural processes of soil development, so that it absorbed the rain and melting snow. There was little or no surface washing. Beneath the cover of vegetation lay nourishing soils of varying depths, created by intricate processes of soil formation through countless millenniums. Nature had balanced income and outgo with an economy sufficient to the needs of this solitude. Then into the valley came Europe's land-hungry millions, men starved for a corner of earth, a patch of ground. With their plows and their axes, their flocks and their fires, they initiated new forms of erosion that proceeded far faster than the ancient processes of soil creation.

Experts on President Roosevelt's Mississippi Valley Committee estimate the losses from soil erosion to be at least twenty times as great as the losses caused by floods. There are large areas, once the most fertile in the whole valley, that have less than twenty years of life. Twenty springs, twenty freshets, and there will remain only the stiff clay subsoil, barren and harsh. There will be completed then the cycle that has already begun: taxes delinquent, farms abandoned, ruin, and the rank growth of underbrush. This is to be the fate of the Eden to which the Clemens family came less than a hundred years ago. For the western half of the drainage basin of the Mississippi it is estimated that annual flood losses amount to $8,879,000, while the minimum annual losses from soil erosion for the same area are $186,070,000, and the maximum, $255,470,000. The implications of these figures cannot be exaggerated.

And yet the brown crest of a flood, swirling and boiling and raging against the levees, will draw newspaper headlines, relief commissions, generous appropriations. The power of the river is dramatized. Pity and terror are invoked by the plight of those who live at the river's mercy in the great delta of the South.

The drama of a Mississippi flood could hardly have been more strikingly displayed, in its effect upon countless lives, than in 1927. Flood gauges stood at record levels. From the high bluffs of Natchez you looked out upon a sea of muddy water; fifty miles, and not a house, not a tree, not a sign of human habitation. Crews of weary men slaved to save homes and fields for a thousand miles along the flooded river, building ramparts higher and higher on top of futile levees. Companies of professional and volunteer rescuers cruised about the inland sea that filled the great valley, in search of survivors. New Orleans was menaced. Rescue parties were just in time to save desperate households marooned on receding islands. Or they were too late, and could only add the names of new victims to the growing list of the dead. Whole communities were wiped out, thousands made penniless overnight. Town warred with town, plantation with plantation, lest one be sacrificed to save the other. The crevasse created by dynamite to save New Orleans was bitterly resented in the flooded regions.

Although in its human implications this was the most fearful flood in the history of the river, the archives of the War Department show that the greatest volume of floodwater was measured on the gauge at Cairo in the spring of 1844. And the crest of the flood of 1882 was nearly as high.

Almost from the time when the army engineeers took over the administration of river work, in 1824, the War Department has favored levees for flood control. Army engineers have defended levees in one congressional skirmish after another. When the levees broke or the river topped them and a great cry rose in the land against the levee system, then the army engineers rushed into the breach. They cited historical precedent. Had not the Nile, five thousand years before civilization ever found the Mississippi, been kept in its banks with levees? And had not levees been used from the time that the first plantations were established along the river? Moreover, what would serve better to keep the untamed Mississippi at least partly in bounds? Since there was no overwhelming answer to this last question, the army engineers went back to their levees.

And they triumphed beyond any question. As never before, they built levees on the lower Mississippi. The process that had begun more than two hundred years ago was carried as near to completion as even the most ardent proponents of the levee system ever dared to hope.

The beginning had been modest enough, although as early as 1727 the colonial governor of Louisiana boasted that the levee before New Orleans was a mile long and eighteen feet wide. One of the conditions of a grant from the king of France required

plantation owners to build levees. In 1743 the planters were ordered to complete their portion of the levee line or forfeit their
grants. In 1815, the year that the Battle of New Orleans was
fought, the river was diked in for 340 miles.

And all this was before the army engineers, those indefatigable
moles had taken charge. In 1822 two young officers started it
with a survey and a report recommending that the entire river
should be diked. With this generous aim the army began work a
few years later. In the decades before the Civil War, Congress
showed such niggardliness that the work scarcely got more than
a start. The moles were eager to dig but there was no money to
pay them. It was only when a president like Zachary Taylor, who
owned plantations that had been flooded in Louisiana, was in
power that the engineers got anything like a sizeable appropriation. Under Taylor, $50,000 was forthcoming for a really com-
prehensive survey and plan of development.

The Civil War and a series of disastrous floods, in 1862, 1865,
and 1874, laid waste to virtually all that man had done, laid the
vast delta open to the caprices of the Mississippi. A strong opposition to the levee system had taken definite shape. The argument
was that the levees caused the bottom of the river to silt up and
that therefore you would have to go on eternally building the
dikes higher and higher until you had not only the rampart itself
but the river, too, far above the level of the surrounding country.
Ignoring this dispute, the army engineers went right on digging,
digging at Congress and digging at the banks of the river.

What gave them and their system supreme authority was the
act creating the Mississippi River Commission. This commission
was composed of three army engineers, a member of the Coast
and Geodetic Survey, and three men from civil life, two of whom
were to be civil engineers. A long line of generals, a president or
two, and other men of great distinction have done service on the
Mississippi River Commission. It was one of the high posts that
an army man might aspire to. The commission has never failed
to get money out of Congress, and it has never ceased to throw
up levees.

How successful it has been is shown by the barometer of appropriations. In 1881 Congress came across with $1 million; in 1882, the year of an extraordinarily high flood, with $4 million. Every year since that time there has been an annual flood-control appropriation. By 1912 six million a year was being appropriated, this for flood control alone. In 1917 Congress gave the sum of $45 million to be spent in not less than five years. How much money has gone into the Mississippi for flood control is a secret that is locked in the archives of the army. But one need not for a moment question the army's boast that no such sum was ever spent for any river before in the history of the world. When one examines the record even briefly, that boast seems a shy understatement.

It was after the great flood of 1927 that Congress was persuaded to adopt a plan that was a plan, the plan toward which the engineers had been advancing for several decades. This calls for a system of levees that shall begin at Cairo and continue to a point below New Orleans, with only minor interruptions. This is not to say that there will be levees on both sides of the river, but for the entire 1,100 miles there will be a dike on one side or the other. And here were delicate decisions for the engineers to make, involving state jealousies, for naturally neither side wanted to be without a dike. Except for those extraordinary floods that recur about every fifteen years, the army engineers swore that this levee system would keep the Mississippi within its banks. It would take more money than there is in the United States, say the army engineers — and this gives even the army pause — to build levees high enough to keep in those exceptional floods. But in such a flood the overflowing water will find its way out of the river as the army engineers intend it to go. It will flood over the areas unprotected by dikes, and if foolish farmers have insisted on planting cotton and building houses there, they will have only themselves to blame, since their government will not only have warned them but will have compensated them for potential loss to this land. These dikes are to cost $325 million to be spent over a period of ten years.

This flood-control act was remarkable not only for the size of the appropriation it granted but for the fact that it did not re-

quire local communities, states, or counties, to make any contribution. It represented a complete victory for the army's ancient
contention that the river is the property of the federal government and that as such, the federal government is entirely responsible for its regulation and control. A report by the army engineers on the flood of 1927 was directly responsible for the
adoption of this point of view in the act. The army argued that
unless the federal government — that is, the army — were
granted complete authority, it would be impossible to achieve
flood control.

So the moles began to dig at a speed that made all their previous digging seem mere play. Altogether they will move more
than twice the amount of earth that was dug out of the Panama
Canal. The money is being spent at a rate of about $40 million a
year, and 40,000 men are employed, most of them on part time,
during the course of each year. Existing levees will be raised
three feet and strengthened throughout the alluvial valley of the
Mississippi, which comprises, in the definition of the army engineers, the Saint Francis, the Yazoo, the Tensas with the Boeuf
and Macon valleys, the Atchafalaya basins, and the alluvial
lands around Lake Pontchartrain. The total area of the alluvial
valley is about 30,000 square miles, and of this total, 20,500 miles
will be protected. In addition to the dikes themselves, numerous
floodways will be built in which the river will be released in extraordinary flood stages. And so, it would seem, the problem of
flood control will be settled for all time. But even the army engineers, knowing the river, do not go that far.

Whether the destruction of the forests at the headwaters of the
streams in the Mississippi system has helped to swell the tide of
successive floods is a question that has been debated with almost
as much passion as the issue of the levees. The army engineers
say, as they say in relation to silt and the river bottom, that man's
interference has made little or no difference in the natural
scheme of things. But there is a somewhat more subtle view than
this.

In the opinion of Raphael Zohn of the United States Forest
Service, in his day the foremost authority in this country, forests

have a complex relation to climate, and in particular to rainfall, underground water resources, and stream flow. While diligent research throughout the world has indicated that forests will not prevent the extraordinary floods that follow exceptionally heavy and prolonged rainfall, the presence of a forest does have a definite influence on the habits of a stream. With the destruction of the forest, the flow is far more irregular, with higher flood levels and longer periods of low water. And the presence of the forest serves to mitigate the severity of even exceptional floods and rarely recurring droughts.

Again and again it has been shown that springs dry up when forests are destroyed; that the secret, little-known relationship between stream flow and underground water is forever altered; that the rainfall is reduced not only over the area where once the forest was, but beyond where the winds that blew over the forest formerly prevailed. The plunderers who stripped the forests of the North with ruthless disregard for the rights of man and nature must, in part, answer for the suffering of the people of the plains during the terrible summer of 1934. We have only just begun to perceive the far-reaching consequences of what was once spoken of, ironically enough, as the conquest of a continent.

There were whole stretches of the upper Mississippi where a man might have waded across without difficulty during the summer of 1934; and the same was true in the summer of 1931. Never before had the gauges of the government registered below the zero level for a summer month. In the seventy-five years that records have been kept there has been no precedent, nothing approaching a precedent, for the low water throughout the Mississippi system. In July of 1931 the low record of 2.0 feet was established at Saint Louis. In July of 1934 the river before Saint Louis stood at 0.6. It was reduced to the stature of one of its minor tributaries and its tributaries were dried up, disappeared from the face of the earth.

How much money has poured out of the national treasury into the Mississippi system only God and a few abstruse statisticians are privileged to know. The statisticians cannot find a simple answer, a single round sum, without years of labor in mountainous files. There is no simple answer. It is, merely, the wealth of Croesus, the accumulated treasure of Aladdin, the riches of Atlantis — all so that the Mississippi might, for a given number of seconds or minutes or hours, flow with molten gold.

The demand for river improvement grew through the 1880s to a sustained chorus. Memorials rained in upon Congress. These demands followed a simple formula: the excessive charges exacted by the railroads worked grave hardships upon producers and consumers; salvation lay in the rivers, which were free to all men. In the day of the river boom had not everyone, or nearly everyone, been prosperous and independent?

Behind this easy formula lay an obscure sense of injustice that was to take deeper and deeper root. The plain people of the Mississippi valley were profoundly aware of some flaw in the system under which they lived. The fruits of their toil were carried off for others to enjoy. And their discontent took many forms, for the most part, futile forms. But no matter what other clamor was in the air there was always the demand that the rivers be restored by act of Congress.

This was an easy tune, which the politicians learned to play loud and long. What lay behind this demand of the plain people of the Mississippi valley, no one understood very clearly. Various groups — shippers, land owners, contractors — soon discovered tangible reasons for pushing river improvement. The War Department, naturally, displayed an increasing fondness for river improvement, for it created both jobs and prestige.

Around the subject of river improvement there accrued a way of thinking as fixed and as final as the movement of the stars in their courses, as rooted and unreasoning as any set of folkways. And yet even after the self-seekers and the special pleaders had championed the cause of river improvement as their own, the discontent, the deep, underlying sense of injustice of the mass of the people in the Middle West remained the sustaining force. That is why Congress has yielded year after year without any examination of what may be behind the ancient outcry, in the name of the rivers, for paternalistic pork.

Certain distinguished economists looked into the whole prob-

lem very seriously and earnestly in the course of a survey of
America's transportation resources. They computed, as nearly as
can be computed, the staggering sums that have gone into the
rivers of the Mississippi system. They looked at all phases of the
American transportation problem. Their verdict, arrived at by
apparently unanswerable logic, was against rivers. But they
failed to take into account the intangible factor — that deep discontent of the people of the Mississippi valley — and that, in my
opinion, in large part invalidated their study. Behind the dry pre-
cision of their logic, their careful rationalization, was human
prejudice and hope.

The demand after 1890 was for the federal government to
widen and deepen the river channels in compensation for past
grievances, so that a balance between the manufacturing East
and the rural Middle West might be more nearly achieved. And
the federal government, since politicians knew from memory the
rhetoric of this familiar theme, responded with an increasing
generosity. No longer was there even the fiction that common-
wealths that would benefit from river improvement should share
a part of the costs. After 1890 contributions by states and counties almost entirely ceased.

A species of river fanatic comparable to the single-taxer came
into being. The cure for all economic ills lay in river transportation. It was the nostrum guaranteed to make the poor rich and
the rich richer. The farmer could ship his produce to market for a
fraction of the rate the railroads charged, and the townsman
would get his manufactured goods from the city at low freight
costs. With unremitting energy these fanatics pushed their cause.
They organized river associations, got river conventions together,
infested Washington. Many of them were motivated by hope of a
personal reward from one source or another. But others burned
with a pure and priestlike zeal. And some who began with the
hope of private remuneration ended with a passion for the cause
unalloyed by self-seeking.

When the Panama Canal was complete and the effect it would
have upon the economic life of the Middle West had begun to be
apparent, the chorus of the river fanatics was raised to a higher

pitch than ever. Here was a new injustice — at the hands of the
federal government this time — to be atoned for by river improvement. Certainly the canal strengthened the case of the river
improver; it forced industry in the middle of the country to compete with coastal industry on terms even more unequal than had
prevailed before. With the completion of the canal it became
possible for a manufacturer in New York to reach a market in
California far more cheaply than could a manufacturer on the
Mississippi River. Rail freight rates, even for a fraction of
the distance, could not compete with the cheap water haul. The
West, the province of the river, was more than ever a dependency
of the East, a ward of New York and Pennsylvania, a mere producer of raw materials, most of the value of which the East absorbed in carrying and processing charges. With this new fuel for
the fires of western indignation the river improvers made rapid
progress.

They had two main objectives. First, they wanted the federal
government to establish a nine-foot channel in the Mississippi
and its principal tributaries — the bolder demanded a channel
from Saint Paul to the Gulf at one fell swoop; more modest advocates were content to take the channel piecemeal. Second, they
wanted the government to start a barge line on the Mississippi
system in order, so they said, to demonstrate to private capital
that river transportation was not only practicable but profitable.

Figures give some indication of the advance. Up to 1890, for
example, the federal government had spent on the Ohio River
approximately $8,482,000. This covered, it should be recalled,
the years when the Ohio was the great highway of the West.
From 1890 to 1910 the cost of new construction is estimated at
something more than $20 million. But this was only the begin-
ning.

In 1908 a special board of army engineers recommended the
creation of a nine-foot channel in the Ohio through a series
of fifty-four locks and dams which would cost an estimated
$63,731,485 plus $5 million for the necessary dredging plant.
River estimates are almost always optimistic. The nine-foot
channel in the Ohio, completed in 1929, cost the federal govern-

ment a little less than $100 million and this does not include maintenance charges during the twenty years of construction nor the cost of terminal facilities provided by cities and private firms. The total for the Ohio, from 1890 to June 30, 1930, according to the best estimates of the army engineers, was $150,205,927. To this must be added $88,141,524 spent upon tributaries of the Ohio, making a grand total of $238,347,451 for the Ohio branch of the Mississippi system. Such a figure seems empty and meaningless, and yet it was money spent, a small part of the government debt on which interest charges never cease.

The river fanatics are able to show, with the aid of the army engineers, a substantial increase in water-borne traffic to justify the Ohio's nine-foot channel. But when the figures are subjected to relatively impartial analysis, the increase is seen to be largely a fiction created to serve a partisan point of view. Since 1925, sand and gravel dredged out of the river in the course of river construction and improvement have been included in the statistics of commercial tonnage. Thus, if a sandbar is dredged out of the stream and the sand is carried two miles below and deposited on the bank, so many thousand tons of sand go to swell the total of river-borne traffic. The army has adopted this method of computation for all inland waterways.

The balance of the traffic, aside from this self-made, self-paid "increase," is for the most part between the coal mines of Kanawha, the Monongahela and the Allegheny, and certain industries in the Pittsburgh area, with a small share passing into the Mississippi to Memphis, Vicksburg, and New Orleans. There is a movement of steel from the great plants at Pittsburgh to river points below, about 20 percent of which goes as far as Memphis. The significant fact is that virtually the whole commerce of the Ohio is between one plant and another, and for the most part between branch plants of the same company.

"The advantage of subsidized cheap transportation on the Ohio River system goes not to the ultimate consumers of iron and steel products but, mainly at least, to the particular iron and steel companies which are so situated as to take advantage of these low water costs." This is the most serious charge in the indictment of the waterway system, a charge which even the river fanatics are put to it to answer.

World War I gave river advocates the chance to gain their second objective. When the railways proved inadequate to carry wartime burdens, the government commandeered all forms of transportation, including minor barge lines then operating on the Mississippi system. Sustained by the clamor of river advocates, the army proceeded to accumulate a fleet of new barges. The War Department operated this fleet until 1924, and then it was turned over to the Inland Waterways Corporation, which had been created by act of Congress to run a regular line on the Mississippi and the Warrior rivers. Besides donating the fleet and a quantity of equipment that went with it, appraised at $10,236,-684, to the corporation, Congress doled out another $5 million in cash as "capital" for this endowed corporation. In return, the government got $5 million worth of Inland Waterways Corporation stock. Major General T. Q. Ashburn, perhaps the most politic and astute general in the army, was put at the head of a civilian operating force, and again, in the view of passionate propagandists, the millennium was at hand.

It was tardy in arriving. In fact, while General Ashburton claimed on paper a net income of $922,871 for the period from June 1,1924 to September 30, 1932, this does not stand the objective scrutiny of the economists. They break down the figures presented by General Ashburn to show instead a net profit of $38,962, and part of this they attribute to interest from an additional $7 million in cash that Congress handed out to the corporation in 1929 and 1930. And they add:

"As a government agency the Corporation has certain cost advantages that would not be enjoyed by a private company, such as free postage and wireless service, free legal services, and government rates on telegrams. There is also free office space to the extent of 2200 square feet. Nor does the Corporation pay taxes on its property assets valued at $24 million, except $8,490 (1931) to the State of Alabama for property in that state. At the low rate of $2.00 per hundred, taxes would amount to $480,000 per year."

Another great national crisis, the Depression, brought the final objective of the river improvers within sight. Victory had been foreshadowed, but as a hope of the distant future, by Herbert Hoover. During the era of prosperity, the great engineer had spoken — the occasion being the completion of the Ohio channel — of the necessity of dredging the entire Mississippi to a depth of nine feet. The cost would be — it was an airy estimate — $800 million, perhaps a little more. Under President Roosevelt, as the Depression deepened, money was forthcoming to begin the reconstruction of the great river.

It will be, when complete, if only for the sheer physical spade work, one of the great engineering projects of all time. The river above Saint Louis will cease to be a river. Through engineering skill it is being converted into a series of lakes in which the flow of the current will be all but stopped. The nine-foot channel will be a reality independent of the weather, a stretch of water seven hundred miles in length and as placid as the Erie Canal. Or so, at any rate, the engineers claim. But river men who saw the Mississippi at unprecedented low levels in the summer of 1934, so low that the Inland Waterways Corporation could not operate on the upper reaches, are frankly skeptical.

Work is going forward at a furious pace the whole distance from Saint Paul to Saint Louis. At the height of operations during the season that ended in the late fall of 1934, there were thirteen thousand men at work. In addition, there was a horde of army engineers and supervisors whose duty it was to keep watch over the private contractors. The Public Works Administration first made available an appropriation of $33,500,000. This was followed by a "second year allotment" of $18 million.

The list of eighteen specific projects that are rapidly taking form reads like the dream of a river improver come true. "Minneiska, Minn. Dam No. 5. contract let for $1,792,198. Dredging contract let for $469,195." "Genoa, Wis. Lock No. 8, contract let for $1,421,763, construction of lock." "Muscatine, Iowa, Lock No. 16, contract let for $1,196,978." "Canton, Mo. Dam No. 20, contract let for $2,194,577."

"One who knows the Mississippi will probably aver — not aloud but to himself," Mark Twain observed, "that ten thousand river commissions, with the mines of the world at their back, cannot tame that lawless stream, cannot curb it or confine it, cannot say to it, 'Go here,' or 'Go there,' and make it obey; cannot save a shore which it has sentenced; cannot bar its path with an obstruction which it will not tear down, dance over and laugh at."

But Mark Twain could never have imagined the scope of this plan as it existed on blueprints in the army engineers' offices in Washington and Saint Louis. Twenty-six major dams, each with its own set of locks, to be built into the upper Mississippi. They were to be roller-type dams, in appearance like huge boilers or cast iron drums, with an open slit in the center facing the stream. Each of a number of individual sections can be raised or lowered at the will of an operator who is to be stationed in a control tower at one end of the dam. Silt, which is such a serious menace to present power and irrigation projects, cannot collect behind this type of dam, it is claimed. The first of these dams was begun at Rock Island, to do away with the rapids that had plagued two generations of pilots and destroyed so many river packets in the days of the river boom.

And what is it that the river advocates, men such as Horace M. Hill and A. C. Wiprud of Minneapolis, Halleck Seaman of Clinton, Iowa, Lackland Macleay of Saint Louis, and Theodore Brent of New Orleans, hope to see accomplished when this engineering eighth wonder is completed? There is no limit to their hopes. Iron ore is concentrated in enormous quantities within a hundred and fifty miles from Saint Paul. Great stores of soft coal lie untapped in the southern Illinois fields. The river will bring them together. Present industrial towns will expand, new ones will spring up all along the river. The Mississippi valley will become the manufacturing center of America. The Pittsburgh district, which was after all only the arbitrary creation of selfish easterners concerned mostly with feeding the railways unwarranted revenues, will dwindle and pass away. So runs the familiar story.

"No one can realize what is at stake here," says Seaman. His is the booming, exultant voice of the prophet. "What a tremendous stake there is! Western railroads are the tail of the kite, subsidiary to great eastern roads, in which Wall Street is primarily interested. Great eastern banking houses control all the railroads — there is simply no discussion about that. And those great eastern bankers are determined that his middle-western country shall always be their fiefdom — paying an enormous tariff in rail rates to those bankers. The water is the way to lick 'em, and we're well on the way to do it."

It is hardly necessary to add that the whole face of the upper valley is being changed, that already there have been profound changes. Gone are the sloughs and the bayous, the remote, lonely inlets that retained through all the years of "civilization" a virginal stillness and peace. Many of them have been drained to straighten the channel and feed the main stream, others will be lost in the big lakes that the new dams will impound. An old river is being twisted and turned and yanked and hauled about to make a new canal. The gaunt skeletons of dying trees, half submerged in newly created lakes, symbolize, as well as anything else, this vast operation.

A project for the Missouri River is of almost equal magnitude. The more ardent proponents of the Missouri, including a governor and a senator or two, foresee great fleets at the wharves of Nebraska and South Dakota towns. Already this project has taken some $67 million of public works money. Fifty million has been allocated for the Fort Peck dam and reservoir in eastern Montana, a colossal engineering feat involving the construction of a huge earthen rampart that will create a lake 175 miles long.

"The Fort Peck dam is being built primarily as a storage reservoir to provide a sufficient flow in low-water seasons to meet the needs of navigation on the Missouri River," said the official announcement. "The dam, approximately 11,000 feet long and its maximum height 245 feet, is located in Valley and McCone counties, Montana, 1,878 miles from the mouth of the Missouri River. This dam alone will provide an adequate flow of water in dry seasons for the entire length of the Missouri River."

What is remarkable is not that so generous a share of the public works appropriation went into the rivers, but that an even larger proportion of the federal subsidy was not spent in this way. For here was a traditional social pattern, the beginnings of a collective enterprise. There were numerous partisans to argue, from long familiarity, the social usefulness of this enterprise. And such convenient and established patterns must have seemed rare enough to those responsible for spending the PWA fund, surveying, as they did, a desert waste of exhausted individualism.

The rail and water argument has never ceased. Although the Inland Waterways Corporation was created with the understanding "that further expenditures of government funds for the improvement of our inland waterways would be useless and should be dropped" if the corporation had not demonstrated at the end of five years that it could operate at a profit, a new lease of life was granted on the plea that the railroads had invalidated the test by unfair competition. Congress in 1928 passed the Denison Act, to compel railroads to cooperate with waterways by joining in through routes and joint rates with a reasonable division of the revenue. And there is official support, from no less a person than Railroad Coordinator Joseph Eastman himself, for the view that the river system is the helpless victim of the railways' machinations. In 1933, in the course of a decision in a rate hearing involving the two ways of transportation, Mr. Eastman reviewed the ruthless destruction of the steamboat trade by the railroads, and added:

> After the railroads swept the inland waterways practically clean of competing traffic, two influences set in. One was a public demand upon Congress for appropriations for the improvement of the waterways, so that they could handle traffic more cheaply and efficiently. The other was a gradual revision of the railroad rate structure to a so-called 'dryland' basis, owing to the absence of water competition. . . . These two influences have brought a return of water competition which had disappeared, and it is progressively increasing.

> This return of competition has so alarmed the railroads that they are ready to go back to the old policy of rate cut-

ting, and have already made several moves in this direction, of which that which is here under consideration is one. If they continue with this policy unchecked, I have little doubt that they will eventually cripple their water competition as they were crippled in days gone by.

Faith in the river system as the source of all good and great things has had a long life. Here is the secretary of war in 1934, speaking to a convention of river advocates ready to cheer a fervent apostle of the radiant future of a long-suffering region: "This is not only the bread basket of the nation but it is the repository of vast deposits of iron, coal, oil, copper, lead, zinc, and unnumbered other raw materials which form the basis of the nation's industrial life. They will come together to create a great industrial empire of free and independent citizens." Cheers, cheers, cheers!

In the mid-term election of 1934, river advocates may have contributed to the Roosevelt triumph but they were only one voice in the chorus. In that year the party in power broke all precedents by gaining nine seats in the House, contrary to the losses that are the normal outcome.

The Public Works Administration has made a large contribution toward the creation of a waterway that is to be the fulfillment of the fondest hopes of the river dreamers. It is happening as FDR seeks every outlet to spend the nation out of the Depression. And nothing could be more appropriate than the great river and the hopes and fears it embodied.

17

The Money Game

The great river may have been tamed, dredged, docked, converted to a canal, but who owned it was still the question in 1978, in a world the prophets of the past could never have conceived. In the view of the visionaries, the railroads — the monsters that had stood in the way of the prosperity and independence of the vast middle region of the nation — were ailing. Planes, trucks, and buses had cut deeply into the near monopoly they once enjoyed. Highways crisscrossing the nation had been built at the cost of many billions of dollars, derived in no small part from the taxing power of the federal government. Airports had come into being with the help of federal largesse.

How did the river, the great canal, fit into this late-twentieth-century picture? The answer came, surprisingly enough, from Senator Pete Domenici of New Mexico. The river was to all intents and purposes the property of the great corporations that used it free of charge while the federal government paid out millions each year — with inflation, closer to a billion dollars — for the upkeep of the locks and dams on the Mississippi system. With the help of two perceptive staffers, Harold Brayman and Lee Rawls, who saw in the issue political rewards for a senator virtually unknown up to that point, Pete Domenici, the Republican senator from New Mexico, set out to bring the corporate giants to heel with a user fee that would pay at least part of the cost the taxpayer was bearing.

While it got comparatively little public attention, what followed was one of the bitterest conflicts in the history of the river system. The issue was money, pure and simple. The corporations — oil, steel, chemicals, a variety of consumer goods — had had a long-standing free ride. Their barges moved from plant to plant, from raw-material resources to manufacturing plants, along a waterway kept in first-rate operation by the federal government. The railroads had long protested the inequity of this free ride, and that protest was ever louder as revenues fell off and the cost of maintaining deteriorating rail lines constantly increased.

The battle began when Pete Domenici put in a bill providing for a user fee, small in the first instance and mounting year by year. Seldom has the Capitol seen such armies of well-heeled lobbyists as marched up the hill to contest in committee hearing rooms and to propagandize in private hideouts. Tempers often flared as witness after witness rolled up the record. At one point, as Domenici was testifying, a bold advocate of the barge lines rose in the crowded hearing room to shout, "Why are you pushing this? It isn't any of your business." Those familiar with Domenici's feisty independence felt that if any further incentive were needed, this provided it. He was outraged that a lobbyist could tell him that the public's business wasn't his business.

This was when the Democrats still controlled the Senate as well as the House, and the Reagan revolution was still well beyond the horizon. As Brayman and Rawls plotted with Domenici to put through the user fee they recognized a key opponent in Senator Russell Long of Louisiana. As chairman of the Committee on Finance, the ultimate authority on all taxation and for that matter on spending as well, he exercised his unrivaled power with the wiles of the good old boy from Louisiana. The chairmanship is only one of the tentacles Long had thrust deep into the Senate structure. With his five terms in the Senate he had acquired a knowledge and a skill making it almost impossible to get a bill past him that he opposed. His fondest concern is the oil and gas resources of his state and the commerce of New Orleans. It was a foregone conclusion that Long would be opposed to Domenici's user bill.

His good-old-boy facade masking his power and his vigilance over the whole legislative process, Long could afford to lie doggo as the lobbyists marshaled their forces on the battlements. The barge lines, virtually all subsidiaries of the great corporations, hauled each year millions of tons of grain, iron ore, and chemicals on the Mississippi, the Ohio, and smaller tributaries. With a remarkably efficient organization, as many as twenty-five or thirty barges were linked in a flotilla pushed by a single propeller-driven craft.

In hearing after hearing the railroads made the case that the right-of-way for the barge lines was free while the railroads paid to maintain their tracks, and that they paid as well a variety of state and local taxes. This difference made it impossible, the railroad spokesmen argued, to compete with the free ride of the barges — the ride being paid for by the federal government at a cost for maintenance alone of as much as $1 billion a year.

In the lobbying battle curious currents beneath the surface now and then came to light. As the conflict continued, money was no concern. Lawyers with lobbying skills, both Republicans and Democrats, got fat contracts. They haunted the Capitol for one side or the other. Surprising transformations occurred. George Smathers, a former Democratic senator from Florida, had been a hired gun for the Association of American Railroads. A personable, smooth-talking type, he had been employed to lobby in favor of a user fee. Switching sides, he joined up with the American Inland Waterways Committee, for a fee that could only be a guess since lobby registration does not require precise figures.

According to one estimate, each side spent at least a half million dollars on bill S.790. Montgomery Ward and the makers of Saran Wrap poured in money on the barge side, while the often obscure subsidiaries of large corporations financed the railroad lobby. At times comic contradictions came to light, all of this, of course, with the public having little or no knowledge of the conflict, or what it might mean in ultimate prices at the checkout counter. U.S. Steel managed to be on both sides. One of their subsidiaries, Ohio Barge Line, Inc., contributed to the fight against the user charge. Another wholly owned Steel subsidiary, the Elgin, Joliet and Eastern Railroad, put out for the railroad side.

Skilled in the ways of the Senate, Domenici's staffers had from the outset prodded the senator to stay with the cause even though at times the head count made it look hopeless. They came up with a strategy they believed was the surest, perhaps the only, way to success as time ran out and Long threatened a filibuster. That was to link the user fee with reconstruction of Lock and Dam 26 at Alton, Illinois. After many years in operation, 26 had all but broken down, and threatened to cause a major slowdown in Mississippi traffic. Many senators opposing a user fee were resolute in their determination that Lock and Dam 26 be rebuilt. The cost to the government would be from $400 to $600 million. Ardent river senators argued that given the inevitable delay in barge operation it was important to get on with 26 as quickly as possible.

S.790 was transformed to link Lock 26 with the user fee. This was an astute move since it presented a difficult choice to the advocates of the free ride for the barge lines, one of whom was Adlai Stevenson III of Illinois. Preparing for his retirement at the end of his second term, he had put his opposition to the user fee at the top of his priority list. Yet he seems to have failed to understand how essential was the linkage, and that was his weakness as the fight went on. Other proponents for the barges, like Republican Senator John Danforth of Saint Louis, were more realistic.

A great deal of influence had been brought to bear to insure passage of S.790. Brock Adams, then secretary of transportation, had become one of the staunchest advocates of the need to bring at least some equity into the rate structure by making barges pay at least part of the cost of their right-of-way. He had persuaded President Carter to favor a user fee, and the president had at one point spent several hours phoning from *Air Force One* to senators he hoped to win over. The initial cost of the 23,000 miles of the river system, the main streams and their tributaries — $3 or $4 or however many billions — had long been written off. It was the maintenance paid each year by Congress that Domenici and the other advocates of the user fee hoped to recover, at least in part.

After months of tugging and pulling on both sides of the conflict, floor debate on S.790 began in the Senate on June 22, 1978. Domenici and his lieutenants, Brayman and Rawls, were in the front row, prepared for what they feared would be a lengthy session. Before the debate had really begun Stevenson put in an amendment calling for an eighteen-month study of the user fee while leaving intact, of course, the authorization for 26. This would have effectively killed the user fee since it was the propitious moment for passage, and after a year and a half no one would remember what it was all about. A complication for Domenici was parliamentary. Senators rushing to vote in response to the buzzer sounding in every office would have to vote nay to kill the amendment since it took precedence. That was a hazard. Domenici and his staffers were worried when they saw Long walk onto the Senate floor in mid-afternoon with the text of what was obviously a lengthy speech and a half dozen books, carefully marked up. Was this the ammunition for a filibuster that would bury the bill?

But with that fine good-old-boy confidence in the outcome, Long rose to say that while he had considered presenting his views *in extenso* (shorthand for filibuster), he had decided that those views were already pretty well known and so he thought the time had come for a vote. The only conclusion was that the old master had accepted a faulty head count. That was obvious as the tally went on. Nays to kill the amendment and ayes were tied. A rare silence settled down on the floor and the galleries as the count went on. And then finally the tally clerk: "The ayes are forty-four and the nays are fifty-one and the amendment offered by the gentleman from Illinois is rejected." Domenici's face is not one to reflect elation, but as he was congratulated by friends and foes alike it came close to that. Passage of S.790 was then a foregone conclusion, and late in the day the vote was seventy-one to twenty.

What followed was a seemingly interminable backing and filling between Senate and House. Jealously guarding their prerogative over all taxation, leaders in the House, conspicuously Al Ullman, then chairman of Ways and Means, held that the user fee was a tax. Between House Speaker Thomas P. (Tip) O'Neill, Jr., and the White House a series of maneuvers went on. O'Neill could tell the House that the president would veto the authorization for Lock and Dam 26 unless a user fee was tied in with it. That may have been the clincher. So the House passed a minor tax measure to which it was hoped the Senate could attach good old S. 790. Approval of both houses was essential as the adjournment deadline drew perilously close.

Once again it was Adlai Stevenson who played a trick card. On a quiet Saturday afternoon when the Senate was almost deserted, preoccupied with moving routine legislation, the senator from Illinois dropped in an amendment authorizing construction of 26 to a pending measure. He assured a senator who inquired that this was just a normal waterways project. When Brayman, skimming the Congressional Record on Monday, discovered what Stevenson had done he exploded. It was deliberate deception. He and Rawls immediately telephoned Domenici, who was campaigning for reelection in a remote corner of New Mexico. You've got to come back or we've had it, they told him.

Domenici took the night flight from Albuquerque and arrived at the Capitol red-eyed and unshaven. By a happy coincidence he ran into Senator Long on the elevator going with Brayman and Rawls to his office. The good old boy was in a beneficent mood, having realized that he could not defeat the user fee. He would not let Stevenson get away with that trick. "Don't you worry," he told Domenici, "I'll see that you get your bill." The way he managed it was a classic illustration of Long's mastery. He had, he said, a few little old bills that had come over from the House. He always kept back a few little old bills, and he'd get one of them out and attach the user fee — Lock and Dam 26 to it.

And that was the way it worked. The Domenici bill was attached to a minor tax measure providing federal tax exemption for gains by certain organizations and individuals from tax-exempt bingo games.

There were a few last minute hitches with adjournment twenty-six hours away. In the House an earnest member from Iowa, Berkley Bedell, rose to say that the proposed tax to be imposed on the fuel used by the barges — four cents a gallon, or $40 million a year — to go into an Inland Waterways Trust Fund, was far too small. It would not begin to recover the costs involved in maintaining the system. Since Speaker of the House Tip O'neill has some of the same skills as the good old boy from Louisiana, the House came up with the required two-thirds majority for a measure sent over from the Senate.

After the Reagan landslide in 1980, the Washington scene was entirely changed. The newspapers in New Mexico had given considerable play to Domenici's victory in the barge fight, which contributed to his reelection in 1978. Beginning his second term in the Senate he was a commanding figure. With the Republican majority the senator from New Mexico became chairman of the Senate Budget Committee. In that office he played an important part in putting through the Reagan budget cuts.

A fee for use of a right-of-way paid for by the federal government was no longer in itself a controversy. It was logical in light of the deep cuts he put through in welfare programs that President Reagan should take it up. He did that in his televised address to the nation in September of 1981:

> When the federal government provides a service directly to a particular industry or to a group of citizens, I believe that those who receive the benefits should bear the cost.
>
> For example, this next year the federal government will spend $525 million to maintain river harbors, tunnels, locks, and dams for the maritime industries. Yacht owners, commercial vessels, and the airlines will receive services worth $2.8 billion from Uncle Sam.
>
> My spring budget proposals included legislation that would authorize the federal government to recover a total of $980 million from the users of these services through fees. That is only a third of the $3.3 billion it will cost the government to provide these services.

Here was a conservative Republican president calling for an end to the bonus that America's largest corporations had cherished for years. Senator Robert T. Stafford of Vermont, chairman of the Environment and Natural Resources Committee, put in a bill to escalate the user fee through 1986. A cosponsor was Senator James Abdnor of South Dakota, chairman of the subcommittee on water resources. But there were delays as the sponsors waited on a report from the Department of Transportation. That report on the various means of transportation and their costs had been called for in Domenici's user-fee bill.

While he was preoccupied with the duties of his chairmanship Domenici also pursued his interest in the user fee. The Stafford bill called for recovery of 100 percent of the maintenance costs. Domenici put in an amendment providing escalation up to 75 percent of recovery.

Needless to say, the lobbyists were as active as ever. The barge lines had two generously staffed organizations, one in New York and one in Washington, and a battery of lawyers, several of whom had been active in the fray from the beginning. In propaganda spread around the country, particularly in areas where barge traffic is important, they spread a new line: the railroads were subsidized; what about those great land grants that meant large fortunes for the men who built the transcontinental railroads? Here was a subsidy far exceeding that which went to the river system. Ably staffed, the Association of American Railroads gave all popssible aid and comfort to those in Congress pushing the user fee.

But the process was bound to be long drawn out. Every delaying tactic was used by each side in the struggle. And the barge lines, with all their political and financial clout, could not be too concerned. Testimony by the Office of Management and Budget showed that the small fee applied under the Domenici bill had produced scarcely half of the estimated $40 million; why, no one seemed to know.

There was a slightly comic turn when the critical issue of the sale of the AWACS planes to Saudi Arabia, part of the largest arms deal ever, was before the Senate. Senator Russell Long, who had not hitherto declared his intention, was reported to be the swing vote. As it turned out, his was not the swing vote since two Republican senators did last-minute quick changes. Long told reporters that morning that he was going to listen to the debate and then decide. This was so contrary to his usual custom that it occasioned no little laughter in the Senate press gallery. In any event, he was one of the fifty-two who gave President Reagan his triumph. And the good old boy was on the side of the powers that might or might not push the user fee to some measure proportionate to the benefit derived by the barge lines. The cynics could believe that he had received a slight hint from those same powers that he did not have too much to worry about.

That this political chess game for high stakes should be the end of the saga of the river I am reluctant to believe. Domenici feels that with the barge lines required to pay for their right-of-way, they will see to it that the river regains something of the character and distinction of another day. I will fall back on Mark Twain: to assume that the stream has been tamed, docked, subdued once and for all is highly dangerous.

What will happen now that commerce moves with a schedule dictated by the big users is hard to imagine. The lock tenders turn up for their shifts with disciplined regularity, well-paid servants of the government in Washington. The Army Corps of Engineers is a dedicated nursemaid, keeping maintenance up to the mark through constant vigilance. But in the sprawling terrain of the river system anything can happen — an unprecedented drought, perhaps, with a disastrous decline in the water resources of the valley.

Certainly it is still too early to write the finish in dollars and cents, and nothing more, after all the turbulence of men and flood and violent encounter. The transformation has been so complete: from the canoes of Nicolet and La Salle to the locks and dams of a canal for waterborn traffic on a scale that even dreamers who foresaw another Golconda on the banks of the Mississippi could never have imagined — four centuries of discovery and conflict, encompassing so much of life and death, joy and sorrow, triumph and tragedy.